NEW GUIDE TO
Babycare

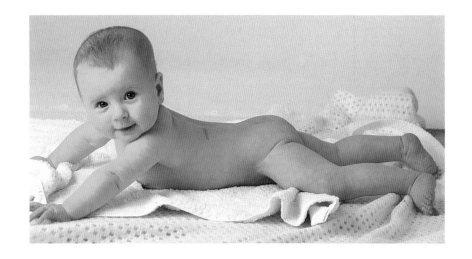

NEW GUIDE TO
Babycare

ALISON MACKONOCHIE

LORENZ BOOKS

A VERY SPECIAL THANK YOU TO ROBIN FOR HIS UNFAILING SUPPORT, TO LUCY AND KATE, WITHOUT WHOM
WE WOULD NOT HAVE HAD CHRISTMAS, AND TO DOMINIC FOR JUST BEING HIMSELF.

This Paperback edition published by Lorenz Books
27 West 20th Street, New York, NY 10011

LORENZ BOOKS are available for bulk purchase for sales promotion
and for premium use. For details, write or call the sales director,
Lorenz Books, 27 West 20th Street, New York, NY 10011;
(800) 354-9657

Lorenz Books is an imprint of Anness Publishing Inc.

ISBN 0-7548-0515-8

Publisher: Joanna Lorenz
Project Editors: Casey Horton, Nicky Thompson
Editor: Elizabeth Longley
Designer: Bobbie Colgate Stone
Jacket Designer: Patrick McLeavey & Partners
Special Photography: Alistair Hughes
Additional Photography: Carin Simon
Illustrations: Ian Sidaway
Hair and Make-up: Bettina Graham
Production Controller: Don Campaniello

Previously published as part of a larger compendium, The Complete Book of Pregnancy & Babycare

Printed and bound in Singapore

© Anness Publishing Limited 1997, 1999
Updated © 2000
1 3 5 7 9 10 8 6 4 2

CONTENTS

INTRODUCTION

A NEW BABY can seem rather overwhelming, especially if this is your first experience of motherhood. Suddenly you are responsible for the care and welfare of a very demanding little person who needs looking after almost 24 hours a day. If you have never fed, bathed or changed a baby you need to learn how to carry out these daily routines. This book looks at basic babycare and explains, in simple terms, everything that you are likely to need to know about caring for your baby during the first year of life.

It is important to take care of yourself too, especially in the days after the birth, so your post-natal care is described at the beginning of the book.

Feeding your baby should be a special time for you both, regardless of whether you are breast- or bottle-feeding in the early months. But when things go wrong, or your baby doesn't feed in the way you expect, it can be difficult to know what to do. Breast- and bottle-feeding are discussed here, along with the latest information on when and how to introduce first foods.

When your child seems unwell it is quite natural to be concerned. Knowing what to do and when you need to call the doctor comes with experience. In the meantime the section on common childhood ailments such as coughs, colds, teething and sickness tells you how to relieve discomfort and when you should seek medical help. There is also a comprehensive first aid section which explains exactly what you should do if your child has an accident.

Caring for your baby will take up a great deal of your time during the first year, so use the daily routines of bathing, feeding and changing as a time to get to know and enjoy each other.

POST-NATAL CARE

Although your new baby will probably give you intense emotional satisfaction, you may well be physically uncomfortable. Your body has gone through many changes during pregnancy and it will take a while for it to return to its pre-pregnancy state.

Six weeks after the birth your doctor will examine you to make sure that everything is returning to normal; this also gives you a chance to discuss any worries you may have. The doctor will take your blood pressure and check a sample of your urine. Your breasts and abdomen will be examined and the doctor will make sure that any stitches have healed properly. You will probably have an internal examination to check the size and position of your uterus and you may have a cervical smear test if one is due.

If your baby was born in hospital, a midwife or doctor will probably talk to you about contraception before you go home. Alternatively, you can discuss this at your six-week check. Don't take any risks; to avoid getting pregnant again you should use contraception as soon as you resume intercourse. It is an old wives' tale that breast-feeding prevents conception.

If you were not immune to rubella (German measles) during your pregnancy, you will probably be offered the immunization before you leave hospital or at your six-week check-up. Ask your doctor if you are at all unsure about your immunity.

Your body

Immediately after the birth your breasts will produce colostrum, a high-protein liquid full of antibodies. Then, after the pregnancy hormones decline, your main milk supply should come in around the third or fourth day. At this time the breasts swell, feel hard, and can sometimes be painful. Bathing them with warm water is soothing, and letting the baby have frequent feeds will also help. This initial swelling subsides after a few days as both you and your baby get used to feeding. However, if you have decided to bottle-feed, your breasts will remain full for a few days until they gradually stop producing milk. Your breasts will probably never be quite as firm as they were before pregnancy, but a well-fitting support bra and exercise will help greatly.

After delivery your abdomen will probably be quite flabby and wrinkled because of slack muscles and stretched skin. Gentle post-natal exercises will help tighten up your abdominal and vaginal muscles, so make time to do them every day. If you feel you're not disciplined enough to exercise on your own, join a local post-natal class.

Following the birth you will have a vaginal discharge which is known as lochia. This will be like a very heavy period for a few days, with the flow gradually getting lighter until it disappears within a few weeks. Use maternity pads or large sanitary towels to absorb the discharge because there is a risk of infection if you use tampons in the early weeks after the birth. Your uterus will take about six weeks to

Your newborn will find your physical presence very reassuring during the first days after the birth. She will also find your smell comfortingly familiar.

Post-natal exercises

Pelvic floor: Lie flat on the floor with your legs drawn up and slightly apart. Close the back passage by drawing it in, hold for the count of four, then relax. Do as often as possible.

Tummy toner: Sit up with knees bent and feet flat on the floor. Fold arms in front. Lean back until you feel the abdominal muscles tighten, hold, then sit up and relax. Repeat several times.

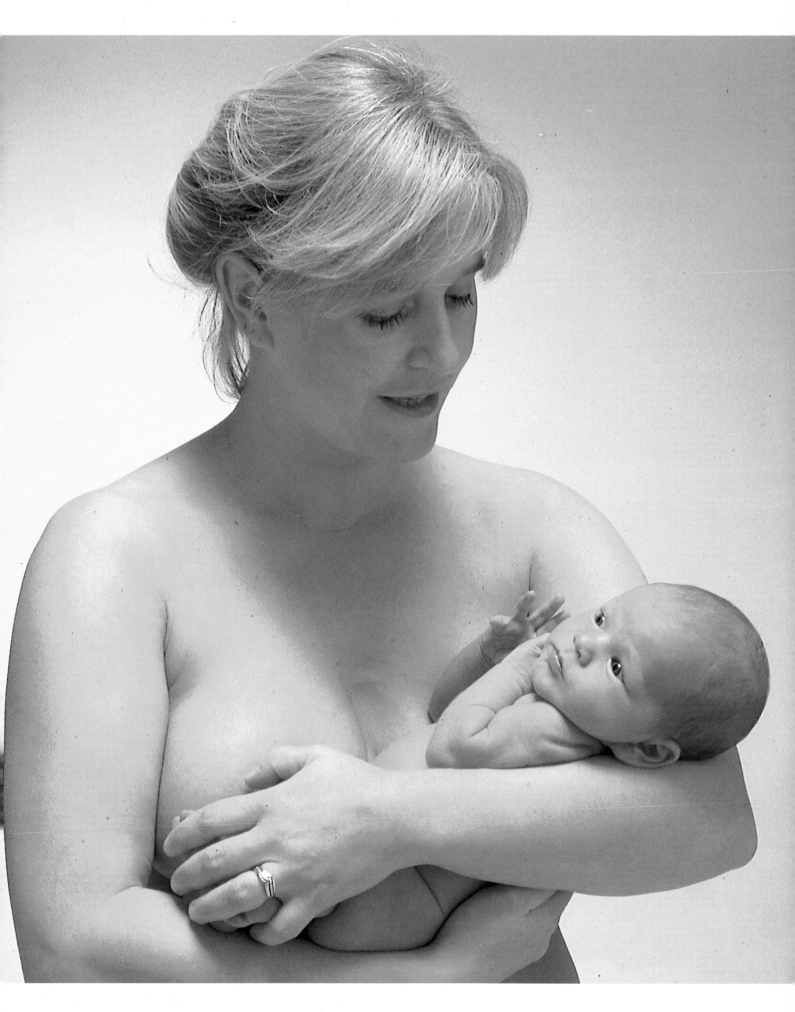

1 *Curl-ups: This exercise will help strengthen your vertical abdominal muscles. Lie on your back with a pillow under your head, your knees bent and your feet flat on the floor.*

2 *Pull in your abdominal muscles and, raising your head, stretch your arms towards your knees. Hold for the count of five and then relax slowly. Repeat several times.*

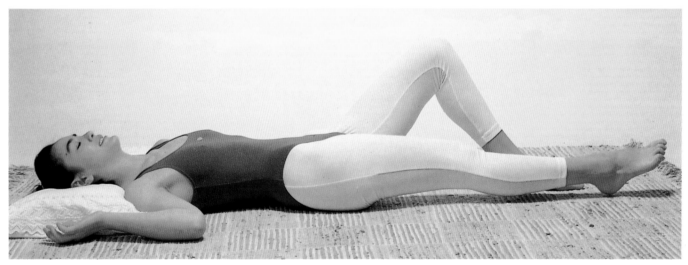

Leg slide: Lie with your head on a pillow with the small of your back pressed against the floor and your knees bent. Gently slide one leg away from your body until it is fully extended, keeping the small of your back pressed against the floor for as long as you can. Slowly draw the leg back towards your body and then repeat with the other leg. Do this several times.

return to its original size. If you are breast-feeding you may feel it contract as you feed the baby.

If your perineum (the skin between the vagina and anus) was bruised during labour, or if you had stitches, you will find that anything that puts pressure on the area painful. Soreness can be soothed with an ice pack (or ice cubes wrapped in a flannel) held against the perineum or by splashing with warm water. Try drying the area with a hand-held hair dryer, set on cool, rather than with a bath towel.

Do not put the dryer too close to your skin, or use it in the bathroom. Adding a cup of salt to the bath water will also help the stitches to heal.

GETTING BACK INTO SHAPE
Despite losing the combined weight of the baby, the placenta, and the amniotic fluid, you will still be heavier than you were before you became pregnant. You may even find that you have to continue to wear maternity clothes for a short while. As your uterus shrinks during the six weeks following the birth you will

lose more weight, but you will need to watch your diet to regain your pre-pregnancy shape. Try to eat regularly and healthily and don't be tempted, because you're short of time, to snack on foods containing empty calories such as sweets and fizzy drinks. If the weight isn't disappearing as fast as you'd like, ask your health visitor for advice. Do not attempt any diet now or while you are breast-feeding – this would simply increase stress as your body is struggling to regain its equilibrium. Doing exercises will help you get

1 *Waist trimmer: Lie on the floor with your arms away from your side, with your knees bent and feet flat. Pull in your abdominals and, with knees together, roll over to the right. Take your knees back to the middle and pause.*

2 *Rest briefly, then pull in your abdominals again and roll your knees to the left, then back to the middle and pause. Keep your shoulders flat on the floor as you roll from side to side. Repeat six times and work up to 20.*

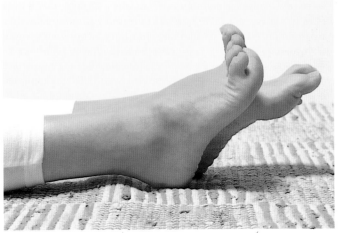

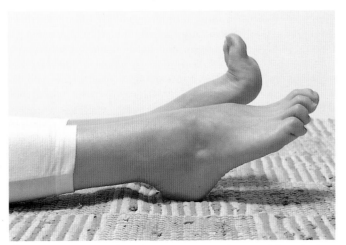

1 *Foot exercises: These will help improve your circulation and are especially important if you are confined to bed. Lie with your legs straight and knees together and bend and stretch your feet.*

2 *Flex one foot, pulling the toes up towards you while pointing the other foot away from you. Repeat, alternating the feet. Do this exercise quite briskly for about 30 seconds.*

Post-natal depression

Two or three days after the birth you may suddenly feel very tearful and depressed. This is commonly called the "third day blues", or the milk blues, because it usually coincides with the milk coming into your breasts. These feelings are caused by all the hormonal changes that are going on in your body and should disappear after a few days. If they don't go away, however, you need to talk to your health visitor or doctor. You may be suffering from post-natal depression (PND) which, if left untreated, can go on for several months. Symptoms of PND include feeling unhappy and wretched as well as irritable and exhausted, yet unable to sleep. You may also lose all interest in food, or find yourself eating too much and then feeling guilty afterwards. PND is one of the most common illnesses following childbirth and it is likely that it is related to the huge hormonal changes that take place at the time of the birth, but it is still unclear as to why it affects some women so badly but not others. If you think you are suffering from PND, don't feel ashamed and don't ignore it. You need help and the sooner you ask for it the sooner you will begin to feel better and able to cope with life again. Post-natal depression is a common condition. Many women are affected by it, and it needs to be treated early on, not ignored in the hope that it will just go away on its own.

your figure back, get you moving again, and make you feel fitter. Those for strengthening the pelvic floor are among the most important post-natal exercises. The pelvic floor muscles support the bladder, uterus, and rectum, so it is vital that their tone is restored after being stretched during childbirth.

TIREDNESS AND RELAXATION
Tiredness goes hand in hand with being a new mother, but you need rest to help your body recover from childbirth. It is tempting to use the baby's sleep times to catch up on chores, but do try to have a nap or proper rest at least once during the day. You and your child are more important than housework, so find ways to cut down the work. Accept offers of help and, if no one volunteers, don't be afraid to ask people.

Another way to cope with tiredness or stress is relaxation, so try using the ante-natal relaxation exercises to help you now. Also a long, lazy bath with a few drops of relaxing oil in the water will work wonders. For a real treat, ask your partner to give you a massage using a specially formulated oil before you go to sleep.

HAIR AND NAILS
The condition of your hair is likely to change during this time. It may become more greasy, or the opposite may happen and it will become noticeably drier than before. You may also suffer an increase in hair loss or your hair may seem a lot thicker than it did before you

became pregnant. Whichever condition applies to you, wash your hair
using a mild shampoo and avoid
rubbing or brushing oily hair too
much as this will only stimulate the
sebaceous glands to produce more
oil. Dry hair should be conditioned
after every wash and, if possible,
allowed to dry naturally.

Your nails are made of the same
tissue as your hair, so if you are having problems with one you are likely
to have problems with the other.
These are due to fluctuating hor-
mone levels and as soon as these settle your hair and nails will return to
normal. Meanwhile, include enough
protein and B vitamins in your diet
because these will help improve the
condition of both your hair and nails.

*Left: A long, lazy bath with a few drops
of oil, such as lavender, in the water will
help you to relax.*
*Below: A stimulating rub with a loofah
brush or mitt will help remove dead cells
on the skin's surface, and will stimulate
the circulation.*
*Below right: Try using some unscented
soap or a soapless cleansing bar if your
skin is very itchy.*

Above: Eating regularly and healthily will help you to regain your pre-pregnancy shape.

CARING FOR YOUR NEWBORN

You may find the first weeks at home with your new baby quite difficult, especially if you are still feeling weak and emotionally down. Don't get upset if the house is a mess; it is much more important for you to spend time with your baby than to do housework. If you are still in your dressing gown at lunchtime don't worry; your baby will not care and it is how he or she feels that matters most at the moment.

Your newborn will seem fragile at first, but is actually quite tough. It is natural to be worried about how to pick your new baby up and hold him without hurting him in any way. Before you pick up your baby make sure that you have his head and neck supported with one hand, then slide the other hand underneath his back and bottom to support the lower part of his body before lifting. Hold your baby firmly against you, either cradled against your chest with one arm still supporting the head and the other holding the bottom and lower back, or cradled in your arms with your baby's head lying in the crook of one arm while your other arm supports his back and legs. Always keep any movements gentle so that you don't hurt or frighten your baby.

THE NEWBORN AT DELIVERY
As soon as the baby is born it will be assessed on the five points of the Apgar Score: heart rate, respiratory rate, colour, activity, and response to stimulation. The baby will be given a maximum of two points for each

category, so if he is pink, active, and responsive the score is 10. The Apgar Score is usually done twice – one minute after birth and five minutes after birth – and it may be done again later if there are any problems.

Your baby will also be weighed and measured by the doctor and will probably receive the first of three doses of vitamin K, by mouth, to prevent a rare bleeding illness which occasionally affects newborn babies. A second dose is given at 10 days and a third at six weeks. Vitamin K is given by injection to very premature babies or those who have had a traumatic birth.

After the birth, the umbilical cord will be cut and a plastic clamp placed about 1-2 cm/½-1 in from the infant's body. Over the next few days

A newborn baby boy's genitals may appear rather big in proportion to the rest of him. This will right itself after a few days.

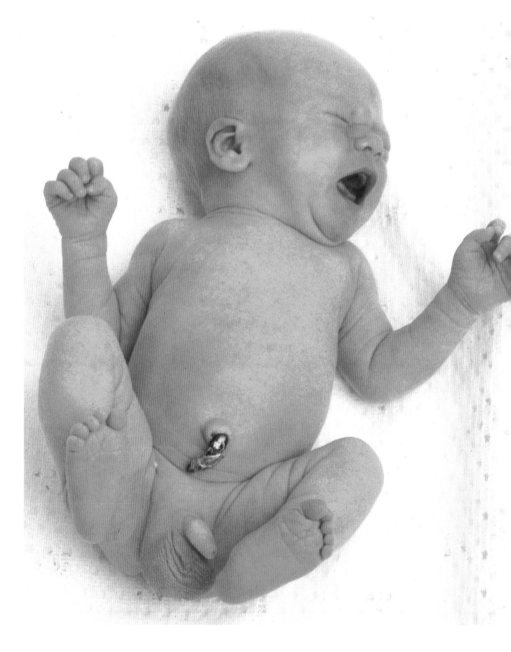

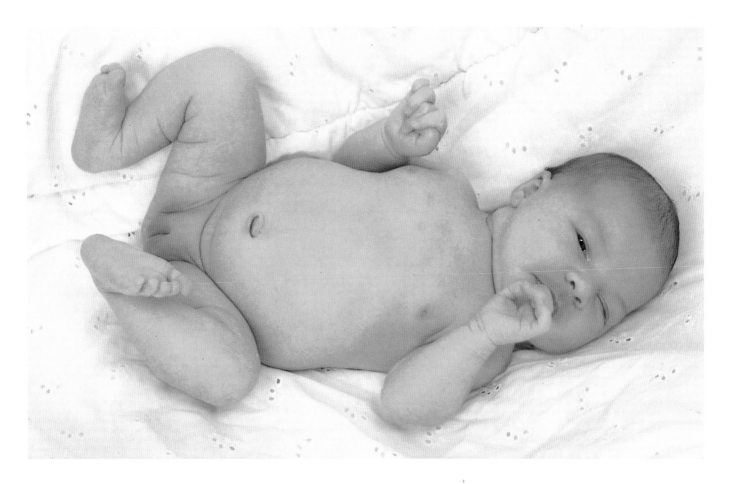

A newborn baby loses the stump of her umbilical cord usually within the first few days after the birth.

the cord will shrivel up and after about a week it will drop off completely. During this time the area around the cord should be kept dry and clean to avoid the risk of infection. Try to let the air get to the healing navel as much as possible so that moisture from wet nappies doesn't affect it.

Your baby has soft spots known as fontanelles on the top of the head. These are the spaces between the skull bones, where they have not yet joined. There is usually a large one on top of the skull and a smaller one further back. They will gradually fuse over the next two years or so. The fontanelles are covered with a tough membrane to protect the brain and you should never press them hard. If you notice a bulge or the skin seems

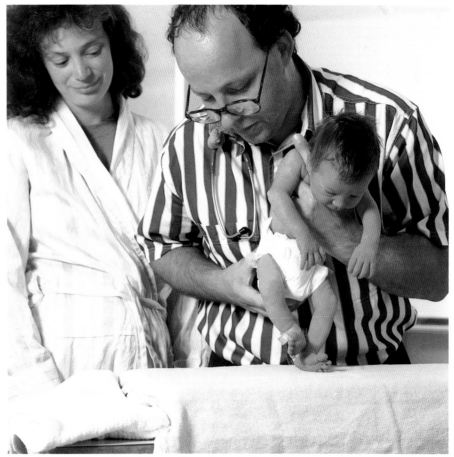

Sometime during the first couple of days your newborn baby will be given a complete physical examination to check that all the organs and limbs are functioning correctly.

15

very tight over the fontanelles you should get in touch with your doctor immediately.

Some babies are born with a lot of hair, others arrive almost bald. Any first hair that a baby has will rub off within a couple of months, but this will be replaced with new hair growth. The new hair may be a different colour.

Most white babies are born with eyes that appear to be blue-grey in colour. This is because melanin, the body's natural pigment, is not present in the eyes until some weeks after birth. Babies with brown or black skins may have brown eyes at birth. If your baby's eyes are going to change colour this will gradually happen over a period of weeks or even months. Although a new baby may cry quite a bit during these early weeks there probably won't be any tears. Some babies don't produce

Babies often scratch themselves accidentally with their nails when they are very young. Scratch mitts will stop your newborn from catching her face with her fingernails.

How to hold your new baby

1 *Pick up your newborn baby by sliding one hand under his neck and head and then placing the other hand under his back and bottom to support his body.*

2 *Lift your baby so that he is cradled against your chest with one arm supporting the head and the other holding the lower back. Holding him close to your body will make him feel secure.*

Right: Touch is very important to a newborn and a gentle massage with a special baby oil can be soothing.

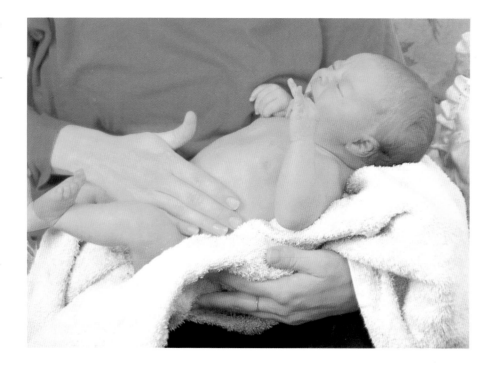

tears until they are six months old – this is not a cause for concern.

Slightly swollen or bloodshot eyes are common in newborn babies. This is caused by pressure from the birth and will disappear within a week or two. The muscles controlling a new baby's eye movements are still very weak so he may look slightly cross-eyed at first. After a month or so the muscles will have developed sufficiently for the eyes to work together. However, even when looking cross-eyed, a baby can focus on things up to 20-25 cm/8-10 in away, so hold your face close when you are feeding or talking.

Enlarged genitals and breasts are common in both boys and girls when they are first born. In some cases the breasts may even ooze a little milk and baby girls can have a slight vaginal discharge. This is caused by your hormones, which are still in your baby's bloodstream. In a few days these effects will disappear.

GENERAL HYGIENE

Young babies often object noisily to being undressed and immersed in a bath full of water, so don't feel you have to bathe your baby every day if the infant is unhappy about it. A top and tail wash every other day is quite sufficient until you both feel more comfortable. Always start by washing the baby's face with cooled boiled water using several pieces of cotton wool. Never use any kind of soap on the baby's face or near his eyes. If you wipe the eyes, use separate pieces of cotton wool for each one and start from the inner corner wiping outwards. A baby's ears and nose

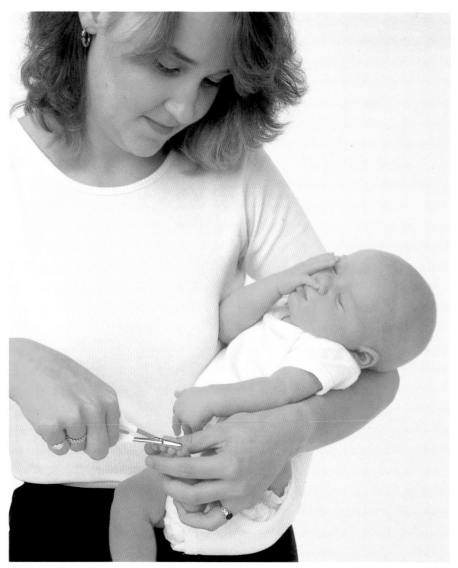

Above: Your baby's fingernails will grow quickly and you will need to keep them short to stop him scratching himself. You may find it easier to cut the nails while your baby is asleep.

are self-cleaning so never try cleaning inside them with cotton wool or buds. Just gently remove any visible mucus or wax. Once you have washed his face you will need to lift up his head and clean the folds of his neck, making sure that you dry the area carefully afterwards. Using

another piece of cotton wool, wash between your baby's fingers and then dry his hands carefully.

When you have finished the top half you need to remove his nappy, wiping away any solid matter before gently cleaning his bottom. You can use lotion to do this, or some warm

water. Once the area is dry, you can apply a barrier cream to help prevent nappy rash.

Cradle cap is very common in the early months and can sometimes continue for a while. Dry white or yellow scales form a crusty cap on the scalp. Rub olive oil, baby oil, or

Topping and tailing

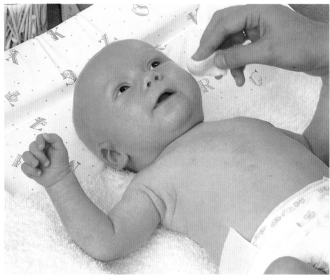

1 *Undress your baby down to his nappy. Using cooled boiled water, and several pieces of cotton wool, gently wash his face. Never use any kind of soap on your baby's face or near his eyes.*

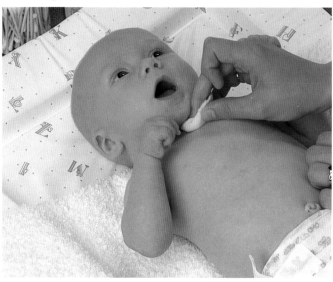

2 *Take a piece of cotton wool and gently lift his chin so that you can wash in the folds of his neck. When you have finished, use another piece of cotton wool and carefully dry between the folds.*

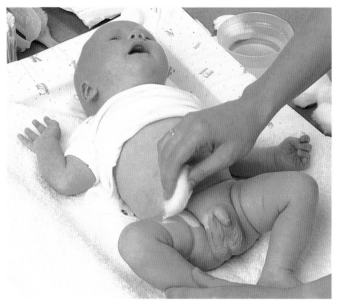

5 *Gently wipe his bottom area with lotion or damp cotton wool making sure that you clean in all the folds and creases of his legs.*

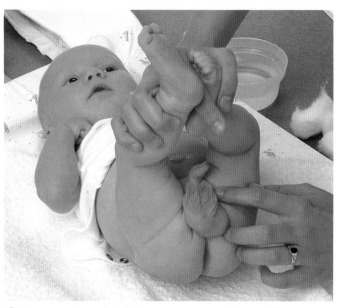

6 *Once you have dried the nappy area, apply a small amount of barrier cream to help prevent nappy rash.*

a specially formulated treatment into the scalp and then comb out the loosened flakes. Wash the baby's head afterwards with baby shampoo and dry thoroughly. You may need to repeat this treatment several times to remove all the flakes. As soon as the condition is under control you will only need to do this once a week. Cradle cap usually disappears by the time a baby reaches about eight or nine months.

A young baby's nails will grow very quickly and if not cut can cause scratches, especially on his face. You should keep his fingernails and toe-nails short by cutting them straight across with a pair of blunt-ended scissors. If your baby objects to this, or you find it difficult to cut his nails while he is wriggling about, try doing it while he is asleep or get someone else to hold him steady while you quickly cut his nails.

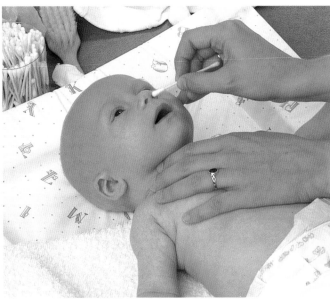

3 *Your baby's ears and nose are self-cleaning, so don't be tempted to clean inside them with cotton buds. Take a dampened cotton bud and carefully remove any visible mucus from his nose.*

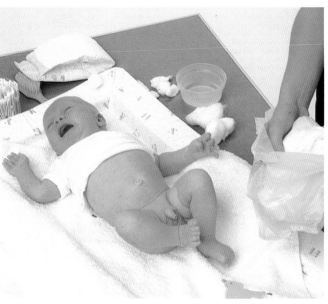

4 *Put your baby in a clean vest and then remove his nappy, wiping away any solid matter with a clean corner before placing the dirty nappy in a bag.*

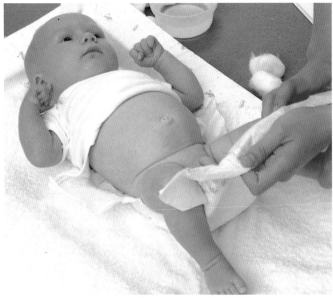

7 *Now that your baby is clean and dry he is ready to have his nappy put on. Place the nappy under his bottom and draw it up carefully between his legs.*

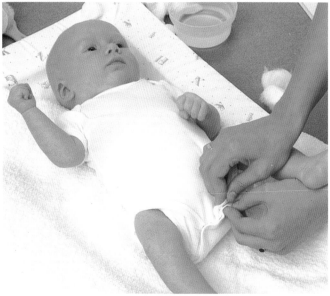

8 *Fasten the nappy securely and once it is firmly in place pull down your baby's vest over the top of it. He is now clean and ready to be dressed again.*

BREAST-FEEDING

Breast-feeding is the ideal way to feed a baby because breast milk is a baby's natural food containing all the required nutrients in the right proportions for the first months of life. But like any new skill, breast-feeding has to be learned and you may find it more difficult than you expected. Don't give up though, because breast-feeding really is best for your baby and for you and, once it is established, it can be a real pleasure. If you are having problems, talk to your midwife or health visitor.

Ideally, you should put your baby to your breast as soon after birth as possible. The sucking will start a reaction that leads to the release of the hormones that cause both the milk to be manufactured in the breast and the let-down reflex, which allows the milk to pass through the breast to the nipple.

Immediately after the birth and for the first few days, the breasts

Getting your baby latched on

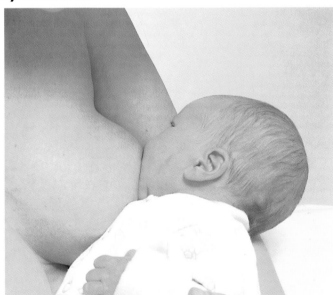

Make sure that your baby's body is in a straight line with your breast so that she doesn't have to turn her head to feed.

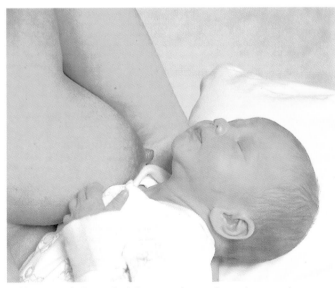

Hold your baby in a comfortable position. Offer her the breast making sure that her mouth is open wide enough.

Allow your baby to feed from one breast for as long as she wants. She will let you know when she has had enough.

produce colostrum, a high-protein liquid full of antibodies. This is followed by the actual milk coming in, which often makes the breasts feel heavy and uncomfortable. This discomfort will soon wear off once breast-feeding has become established.

At the first stage of a feed your baby gets foremilk from the breast; this has a high water content to satisfy thirst. Foremilk is followed by calorie-rich hindmilk which satisfies your baby's hunger and helps her to grow. To make sure that your baby always gets the hindmilk, you should allow her to feed for as long as she wants from one breast before you offer her the other one. If your baby has had enough when she has finished feeding from one breast, remember to start with the other breast at the next feed.

Your breasts produce milk in response to your baby's feeding, so the more your baby feeds the more milk you will produce. By letting your infant feed for as long as she wants you should be able to produce the amount of milk that is needed.

FINDING THE BEST POSITION
Finding the position which best suits both you and your baby is one of the most important factors for successful breast-feeding, so don't be afraid to experiment. Immediately after the birth, when you are still sore, you may find that sitting on a low chair with plenty of soft cushions is more comfortable than sitting in bed. You can raise your knees slightly by resting your feet on a low stool, or put a pillow on your lap to raise your baby and cushion your abdominal muscles.

Hold your baby so that her body is in a straight line with your breast so that she does not have to turn her head to feed. Sit up straight and lean

Breast-feeding techniques

Aim the nipple towards your baby's nose and allow her to take it into her mouth herself. When supporting your breast try not to apply pressure which can block the milk ducts.

Your baby may try to hold your breast or simply clench and unclench her fists while feeding. Her ears will move as she swallows.

When you want to remove your baby from the breast, insert a finger into her mouth to release the suction.

Advantages of breast-feeding

• Breast milk is designed especially for babies and it contains all the nutrients your baby needs. It is always available, at the right temperature, and it is free.

• Breast milk is easy for your baby to digest, so she is less likely to suffer stomach upsets and constipation.

• Breast milk contains antibodies which will help protect your baby against some infections.

• Breast-fed babies are less likely to develop allergies.

• Breast-feeding will help you get your figure back more quickly.

will let you know when she is hungry and your milk supply will be regulated by supply and demand.

EXPRESSING MILK

Expressing milk allows someone else to feed your baby with your breast milk. You can express milk with your hands or you may find it easier to use a breast pump. The best time to express is when you have the most milk, which is either in the morning or, once your baby has dropped her night feed, it may be in the evening. Milk can be expressed from your breast and kept in a sterile container in the refrigerator for up to 48 hours, or it can be frozen and kept for up to six months. Any feeding equipment or containers you use must be sterilized.

BREAST-FEEDING PROBLEMS

If you are concerned that you are not producing enough milk, breast-feeding more often will automatically increase your supply, so don't be afraid to let your baby suck for as long as it is comfortable.

To bring up any wind, either during the feed or once she has finished feeding, lay your baby across your knees and stroke her back gently.

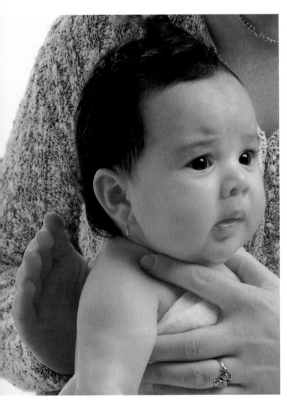

You may prefer to wind your baby by sitting her upright on your knee, supporting her head, and gently patting her back.

slightly forward so that the nipple drops into your baby's mouth. Make sure that she is then properly latched onto the breast. This means that your baby takes as much as possible of the areola (the dark area surrounding the nipple) into her mouth, along with the nipple. The milk ducts lie just under the areola and your baby's sucking action on these effectively draws the milk from the breast. You may well be told to check that your baby's nose is not pushed against your breast so making it hard for her to breathe. However, if your baby is positioned properly, she will be able to breathe easily.

There is no set pattern for feeding. Some babies want to be fed every couple of hours, others can happily go for four to six hours before requiring a feed. Your baby

You may have a sleepy baby who needs to be woken for a feed. If your baby needs encouragement, gently brush her mouth with your nipple but don't force it into her mouth. Your baby may fall asleep at the breast after a feed but this only means that she is contented, well fed and doing all right.

Breast-feeding may hurt during the first few weeks because your milk supply has to become established and your nipples are not yet used to your baby's sucking. If the discomfort persists, however, then the positioning of your baby on the breast may not be right and you should experiment. Also check that your baby is latched on properly. If not, your baby may just be sucking the nipple which means she won't be getting enough milk and the more she sucks the more painful it will actually become.

You may experience engorged breasts. This is when your breasts become over-full and painful. Feeding your baby frequently will help and you can ease the swelling by bathing your breasts with warm water or having a hot bath. Smooth out some milk with your fingers, stroking the breast downwards towards the nipple.

If you experience a shooting pain when your baby sucks, you may have a cracked nipple. If your baby is in the correct position even if your nipples are sore, they shouldn't hurt when you are feeding, so check your positioning. Keep sore nipples clean and dry and let the air get to them as much as possible. A nipple shield which fits over your nipple may help, but don't wear it for more than a day or two. Occasionally sore nipples can be caused by thrush in a baby's mouth. If you think this may be the case, discuss the problem with your doctor.

Finally, some nursing mothers can develop a condition called mastitis. This is an infection of the milk ducts and your breast will be inflamed, hot, and flushed in places. Bathing your breast in warm water, or holding a cold flannel against it, will help to ease any discomfort. You may also need a course of antibiotics to clear up the infection, so consult your doctor.

Sore, cracked nipples and mastitis are usually caused by your baby sucking just the nipple. Make sure your baby takes the nipple and surrounding area well into her mouth when she is feeding.

Breast-feeding equipment

Although no equipment is essential, there are some items which will make life easier, such as feeding bras. There are other things that you may require if you decide to express milk so that you can bottle-feed occasionally. You will need:

• At least two well-fitting cotton nursing bras which allow access to a large area of the breast when your baby is feeding.

• Breast pads for use inside the bra to absorb any leaks of milk.

• Nipple shields to protect your sore nipples.

• Breast shells to fit over the nipple and collect excess milk.

• Breast pump, bottles, and teats.

• Sterilizing equipment if you intend to express breast milk.

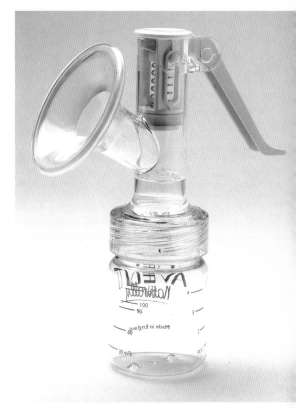

Breast milk can be expressed by hand, or using a manual breast pump like this. Electric pumps are also available.

Various accessories may help with breast-feeding. Breast pads will absorb any leakage, freezer bottles can be used to freeze breast milk, and nipple shields will protect sore nipples.

BOTTLE-FEEDING

If you decide to bottle-feed you should be content with your decision. Do not feel guilty, or think that you are giving your baby second best. Such feelings will only take away the pleasure you should get from feeding your baby. Make the most of each feed by settling comfortably and giving your baby all your attention.

FORMULA MILKS

Formula milk has been specially produced to provide all the vitamins and minerals your baby needs. Most formula milk is made from cows' milk, which has been specially treated to make it easily digestible, and its nutritional quality is as near to that of breast milk as possible. There are several brands to choose from and the midwife will be able to advise you. If your baby is known to have a lactose intolerance, or there is a very strong family history of allergies that are connected to cows' milk, you may be advised to use an alternative to regular formula milk. Often this is a soya-based milk, but others are available. It is important that these alternatives are only introduced if recommended by your doctor.

Formula milks are available in powder forms, which are made up with cooled boiled water. It is important to follow the instructions on the tin or pack because the amounts have been carefully calculated to make sure that a baby gets the correct balance of nutrients. Never be tempted to add more powder than is recommended because feeds that are too strong can be harmful to your baby. Ready-prepared formula milks are also available in cartons and bottles. Ready-prepared formula is more expensive than powdered milk but it's useful when you are out with your baby.

HOW TO BOTTLE-FEED

Prepare the formula milk according to the instructions, making up enough for 24 hours. Store the bottles in the refrigerator until needed

Feeding equipment

All feeding equipment needs to be kept scrupulously clean. Bottles and teats should be washed out immediately after use and then sterilized thoroughly before you make up the next batch of feeds. You will need to have:

• Enough bottles, teats, and caps to enable you to make up feeds for a 24-hour period.

• Sterilizer – there are four main ways of sterilizing feeding equipment: the chemical method, using a container filled with sterilizing solution; an electric steam sterilizer; a microwave steam sterilizer, or boiling on the stove.

• Bottle brush for cleaning inside all the bottles.

• Sterilizing solution or tablets for chemical method.

• Bottle warmer – this is optional, but can be very useful, especially when doing night feeds.

A bottle warmer is useful at night.

Sterilizing equipment for bottles.

A microwave steam sterilizer.

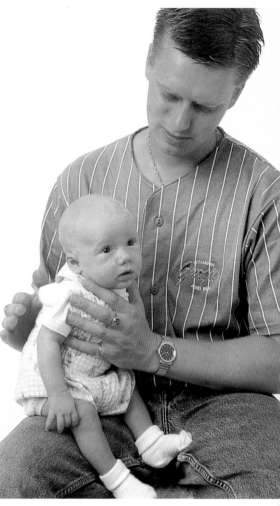

Bringing up wind is something a father can do whether you breast- or bottle-feed.

Feeding should always be a special time for a baby as it helps him bond with the people closest to him. Here a father takes his turn at bottle-feeding.

An older baby may prefer to hold the bottle himself, but he will still need to be cuddled and you should check that the teat is always full of milk.

and make sure that any unused formula is thrown away after this time. Never reuse leftover milk because it is a potential breeding ground for bacteria. Some babies are quite happy to take their bottles at room temperature but if yours prefers warm milk, heat the bottle either in a normal bottle warmer, or by standing it in a jug of hot water. Always test the temperature on the inside of your wrist to make sure that it isn't too hot before giving the bottle to your baby to drink.

Check that the milk is coming through the teat at the right speed. If your baby is having to work hard to get the milk, the flow is too slow and you need a teat with a bigger hole. If, on the other hand, your baby seems to be gulping a lot and the milk is leaking out of the corner of his mouth, the flow is too fast and the teat should have a smaller hole. If the teat flattens while you are feeding, pull it gently out of the baby's mouth to release the vacuum, then insert it again.

All your baby's feeding equipment must be thoroughly washed before sterilization.

Chemical sterilizing

1 *After washing the equipment fill the sterilizing unit with cold water.*

2 *Add sterilizing tablets to the water and place the bottles, teats and caps in the unit.*

3 *Check bottles are filled with water, then place tray in unit. Leave for time specified.*

Electric steam sterilizer

1 *Wash and rinse the feeding equipment and then place it in the sterilizing unit.*

2 *Add water, taking care to follow the manufacturer's recommendations.*

3 *Place lid on unit and switch on. The steam destroys any bacteria present.*

Making up a formula feed

1 *Fill the bottle with the correct amount of cooled boiled water. Never use water that has been boiled more than once.*

2 *Using the scoop provided, measure the required amount of milk, levelling off each scoopful with the back of a knife.*

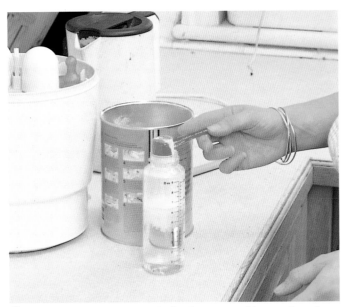

3 *Add powdered formula to the bottle. Never add extra formula as this can make the mixture too concentrated and could be harmful.*

4 *Secure teat and place lid on bottle. Shake until the powder has dissolved. Check the milk temperature before giving it to your baby.*

You may want to encourage feeding by stroking the teat across your baby's mouth. Once his mouth has opened, place the teat between his lips and your baby should start sucking. Keep the bottle tilted so that formula fills the teat completely and your baby doesn't suck in air, which can cause wind. Never leave your baby to feed from a bottle on his own because he could vomit and choke. Don't add solids such as rusk, cereal, or baby rice to bottle feeds – this could cause choking.

The amount of milk your baby needs at feeds will change as he gains weight. At first he may take only a couple of ounces but this will increase. Your health visitor will give you a growth chart to check on progress.

Wind can sometimes be a problem, so try stopping halfway through a feed and wind your baby by holding him against your shoulder, or propping him up on your lap while you rub his back. You may want to do this after the feed has finished as well. The baby may bring back a small amount of milk during or after a feed; this is called possetting and is quite normal. If the vomiting becomes frequent or violent, you need to consult your doctor.

INTRODUCING SOLIDS

Once milk alone no longer satisfies your baby you will need to start introducing solids into her diet. This can be any time between four and six months of age – in general, babies younger than this shouldn't be put on solids. Your baby will let you know she is still hungry by wanting more after the feed is finished, or she may start chewing her fists. A baby may also begin to demand feeds more often and if she normally sleeps through the night, you may find that she starts waking up early wanting to be fed.

Breast and formula milk give babies all they require for the first six months so you don't have to worry if your baby seems satisfied with milk alone until this age. By six months of age, your baby needs the additional nourishment provided by solids, and she also needs to learn how to eat.

How to start

First solids are really just tasters to get a baby used to different textures and flavours; the main nourishment will still come from breast or formula milk. The first food should be bland and smooth, like baby rice mixed with either cooled boiled water, or formula or breast milk. To begin with offer a small amount on the tip of a clean spoon, midway through a feed, once a day. Once your baby has accepted this, you can introduce a small amount of fruit or vegetable purée, for example, banana, potato, or carrot (with no added salt or sugar), mixed with formula or breast milk.

As soon as your baby has got used to taking solids off a spoon, you can begin to introduce new foods and other solids at a second meal. If your baby obviously doesn't like the taste of something don't force matters. Try another food and reintroduce the rejected food at a later stage. At first the baby will simply try to suck anything off the spoon. But it won't take long to master getting the food off the spoon and into the back of her mouth. Once your baby can do this she will be able to cope with lumpier textures, so you can begin to mash rather than purée food. Your baby will also be able to enjoy a wider variety of tastes and textures.

Advanced Feeding

By six to nine months, you can introduce food combinations such as baby cereal and fruit, or egg yolk and tomato – remember to remove the seeds from the tomato and to cook the egg thoroughly. Food can be lumpier and more solid so that it encourages your baby to start chewing. Try mincing or mashing the food with a fork.

At nine months and over, your baby is likely to be on three meals a day as well as milk, unsweetened diluted fruit juice, or water. Giving your child food at grown-up meal-

Making your own purée

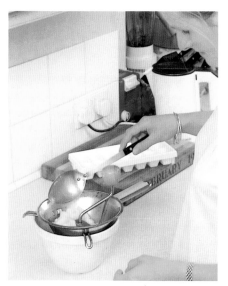

1 *Steam the fruit or vegetable until it is thoroughly cooked and soft, then place it in the food mill or blender.*

2 *Without adding any sugar or seasoning, blend to a smooth consistency then remove a portion for your baby.*

3 *Pour the remaining purée into an ice-cube tray to freeze in baby-size portions. Label and use within one month.*

times will encourage her to learn social skills by watching others. As her appetite grows you can gradually increase the amount given at each meal. Offer finger foods such as slices of peeled apple, and banana; this will encourage her to feed herself. Always stay with your child while she is eating in case of choking.

As with younger babies, don't force unwanted foods; your child may simply not be ready for that particular taste. Don't ever fight over it. Take the food away, but don't offer alternatives or provide snacks between meals or let the child fill up on drinks, especially non-nourishing drinks, such as squash.

THE VEGETARIAN BABY

The principles of weaning are the same as for a non-vegetarian baby with the first solids being cereal, puréed fruit, and vegetables. However, vegetarian diets tend to be high in fibre and too much fibre is not suitable for young babies. And it can also interfere with the absorption of minerals such as calcium and iron. So your child will require a combination of cereals, milk, and vegetables which contain the right balance of energy and other nutrients for healthy growth. The diet will also need to include iron-rich foods such as dried fruit, fortified breakfast cereals, bread, lentils, eggs and green leafy vegetables. Vitamin C helps the absorption of iron from vegetables so you should give fresh orange juice, fresh fruit, or raw vegetables with every meal.

A vegan diet excludes milk and all dairy products, as well as meat and fish, and it may be unsuitable for babies. If you are considering a vegan diet it is essential that you talk to your health visitor or community

Equipment

First foods need to be puréed, preferably using a blender or liquidizer, although a sieve and spoon will achieve the same results. As your baby gets older and is able to cope with lumpier foods you can use a fork to mash the food. Your baby should have his or her own feeding utensils, which you will need to keep very clean.

To prepare and feed your own puréed foods you will need:

• Blender or liquidizer.
• Unbreakable bowl, spoon, and feeding cup.
• Bib (preferably two or three) and several face cloths.
• Ice-cube tray or similar for freezing small portions of purée.

Use an unbreakable bowl, plastic teaspoon and feeding cup when weaning your baby.

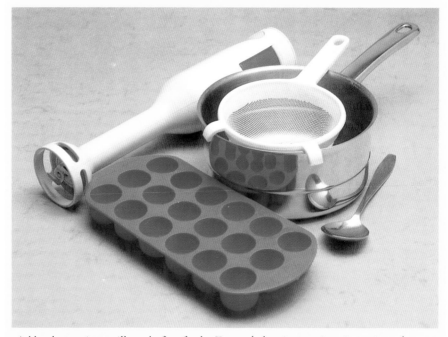

A blender or sieve will purée first foods. Freeze baby-size portions in an ice-cube tray.

Left: By eight months a baby will be enjoying finger foods. At first he will examine the food, squashing it between his fingers as he explores its texture. Right: Once he's examined the food he will probably concentrate on trying to get it into his mouth.

Below right: Using both his hands to help him, he eventually manages to get the food into his mouth. These are the very early stages of how a child learns to feed himself.

dietician before beginning to wean your baby onto solid food.

BABY FOODS

You can make your own first foods by puréeing ripe fruit or vegetables. Remove the skin and any seeds or stones, then boil, steam, or microwave until thoroughly cooked. Allow the cooked fruit or vegetable to cool, then purée. Fruits with seeds such as strawberries will need to be sieved. Make a batch of purée, and freeze in small portions for convenience. Reheat thoroughly before use and allow it to cool before giving it to your baby. When your baby is older and has progressed to lumpier, mixed foods she can eat the same foods as you, but remove a small portion for your baby before you add any seasoning or sugar.

Warming food for babies in a microwave is not recommended because it can result in uneven heating which could scald the child's mouth. If you have to use a microwave, stir the food well after cooking to ensure the even distribution of heat and allow it to stand for at least one minute. Check the temperature again before offering the food.

The alternative to home-made baby food is to choose from the prepared baby foods that are widely available. One of the

Choking

If your baby chokes while eating try to hook out the obstruction with your finger (being careful not to push it further in) while gently slapping on the back. If this doesn't work, lay your baby face downwards with her chest and abdomen lying along your forearm and your hand supporting her head. Then slap the infant gently on the back to dislodge the obstruction.

main advantages of prepared baby foods is that they are quick and convenient. They have been formulated to make sure that, in conjunction with breast or formula milks, a baby receives a nutritionally balanced diet. Available in jars, packs, and tins, there are commercially prepared baby foods available for each stage of weaning. Check the labelling for the age range for which it is suitable and, if you wish, whether it is acceptable for a vegetarian diet.

Introduce new combinations of prepared baby food with the same care as you would home-made food. Different food

combinations contain several ingredients, some of which may be new to your baby. Always place the amount you require in a dish rather than feeding straight from the tin or jar. The digestive substances in your baby's saliva can find their way from the feeding spoon into the container, which can make any remaining food unsuitable for another meal. Once tins and jars are opened,

they should be stored covered in the fridge and kept for up to 48 hours.

FOODS TO WATCH

You must think carefully about the foods you introduce to your baby's

Always feed your baby her food using a plastic spoon. Keep the dish away from her until she learns not to put her hands in it.

diet. Some must be avoided altogether; others simply need special care in their preparation.

High-fibre foods Babies and young children shouldn't be given high-fibre foods such as bran because their digestive systems are too immature to cope with them.

Salt Never add salt to any food that your baby is going to eat. An infant's system can't cope with more salt than is found naturally in food. Remember too that some products, such as crisps, are usually quite salty, so you need to be aware of any salt intake from these foods.

Sugar Sugars occur naturally in fruit and vegetables so you should never add sugar to your baby's food or drinks as this can lead to tooth decay later and the possibility of obesity. Some manufacturers' pre-pared foods may contain sugars, so read food labels: sugars may be listed as glucose, sucrose, dextrose, fructose, maltose, syrup, honey, or raw/brown sugar.

Additional fats Babies shouldn't have much additional fat added to their food – although the occasional knob of butter added to mashed potato will do no harm.

Nuts Whole nuts should never be given to a child under five years of age because of the risk of choking. Nuts that are finely ground may be given to children over six months.

Spices Strong spices such as chillies, ginger, and cloves are not suitable to be given to babies.

Eggs Eggs should always be cooked until solid. Since eggs can also cause allergic reactions, start by offering a small amount of well-cooked yolk. Egg white is not recommended for babies under 12 months.

FOOD ALLERGY

If either you or the baby's father have a family history of food allergies, eczema, asthma, or hayfever, your baby may have an intolerant reaction to the following foods: wheat, oats, and barley cereal; citrus fruits, eggs, nuts, and fish; dairy products, including cows', goats' and sheeps' milk. Intolerance to cows' milk is usually the result of an allergy to one of the proteins in milk or an intolerance of lactose (milk sugar). When you buy commercially manufactured food, always check the ingredients for any foods that may cause an allergic reaction.

Symptoms of food intolerance or allergy include diarrhoea, vomiting

Drinks, other than breast or formula milk, should be given in a feeder cup from the age of six months.

At around one year a baby will be able to manage finger food and a feeder cup without help. Never leave your baby alone when he is eating in case he chokes. Give drinks at the end of a meal or they will fill your baby up before eating.

after eating, or occasionally blood in stools. In extreme cases the reaction can be a generalized blotchy skin rash which occurs within an hour or so of eating the food. Your child's lips may also become swollen, the eyes puffy, and breathing a little wheezy. If breathing becomes restricted you will need to get medical help immediately. The blotchiness and swelling will disappear quickly but it should always be reported to your health visitor or doctor. These extreme responses to an allergy are rare, but may occur from time to time; if they do you should avoid that particular food.

If your child shows an intolerance to any food it is important that you seek advice from your health visitor or doctor. It may be that you need to change your child's diet, but this should always be done with the advice of a health professional.

MILK AND OTHER DRINKS

As the amount of food increases, your baby's intake of milk will decrease. However, the recommendation is at least 600 ml/1 pt of breast, formula, or follow-on milk (after six months) a day, until the baby is one year old.

Follow-on milks have been produced to help meet the nutritional needs of growing babies from six months to two years. They contain more iron than other milks, plus a healthy balance of other nutrients.

In the past cows' milk was introduced into the diet at around six months, but it is now thought that it is unsuitable until the baby is at least one year old. This is because cows' milk is low in vitamins like C and D, and is particularly low in iron, all of which your baby needs for healthy growth. After a year full-fat milk should be give to the under-fives as

Vitamin drops

If you are breast-feeding, it is recommended that vitamin supplements are given to children from six months. Bottle-fed babies do not usually require supplements until they switch to cows' milk at a year old. These vitamin supplements should be given to children up to the age of five. They are available from your health visitor at the baby clinic or you can get them from the pharmacist.

it provides energy, protein, and calcium, even though it has more saturated fat than breast or baby milks.

Reduced-fat milks are not suitable as they are low in calories and vitamins. Skimmed milk should not be given to a child until she is at least five years of age. However, if your child has a good appetite and varied diet, you may offer semi-skimmed milk at two. Always check with your health visitor first.

If your baby seems thirsty and you are still breast-feeding, your milk will provide all the liquid needed. Otherwise, offer cooled, boiled water between feeds after the age of four weeks. Try giving your baby these additional drinks from a teaspoon; this will make the idea of a spoon familiar before you start weaning onto solids. From the age of six months, any drinks other than breast or formula milk should be offered from a feeder cup.

Any water you give your baby needs to be boiled and cooled until the child is at the age when you no longer sterilize feeding equipment. Only use boiled water or bottled water sold specifically for babies – never make up a feed with, or offer your baby, bottled mineral water.

NAPPIES

Nappies are produced in a variety of types, styles, and sizes, but the basic choice is still between disposable and towelling nappies. Ideally, you should decide which type of nappy you are going to use before your baby arrives. You will need to take into account a number of factors: your lifestyle, the amount of time and money you have available, and the type of washing and drying facilities you will be using.

CHANGING

Whichever nappy you choose, the techniques required for changing and cleaning a baby's bottom are the same. You should change your baby whenever he is wet or dirty. The number of changes may vary from day to day, but generally you will have to change your baby first thing in the morning, after each feed, after a bath, and before bed at night. Get everything you need together before you start so that there is no reason to leave your baby unattended while you are changing the nappy. Make sure that the room where you are changing your new baby is warm and free from draughts. Lie your baby on a folded towel or changing mat, placed on the floor, a table, or on the bed, making sure that a

---

Folding towelling nappies/Triple absorbent fold

This is particularly good for newborn babies because it makes a small, neat shape while giving extra absorbency between the legs.

1 *Fold the nappy into four sections with the two folded edges nearest you and to your left.*

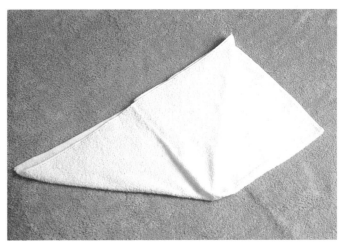

2 *Pick up the top layer by the right-hand corner and pull it out to make a triangle.*

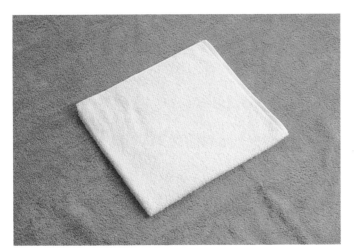

5 *Fold these layers over again to make a thick central panel.*

6 *Place a nappy liner over the top of the central panel.*

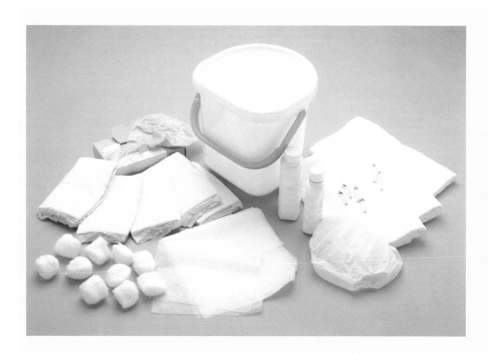

Changing equipment:
• Changing mat or towel.
• Clean towelling nappy, nappy liner, pins, plastic pants. Or a disposable nappy.
• Baby lotion or wipes, cotton wool.
• Bowl of warm water.
• Barrier cream.
• Bucket for dirty nappy or a plastic bag for a disposable nappy.

3 *Turn the nappy over.*

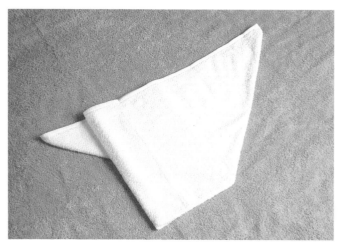

4 *Fold the vertical edge into the middle by a third.*

7 *Bring the middle fold between the legs, then fold one corner across your baby's stomach and hold while you bring the second corner across. Pull taut and then pin all three layers together.*

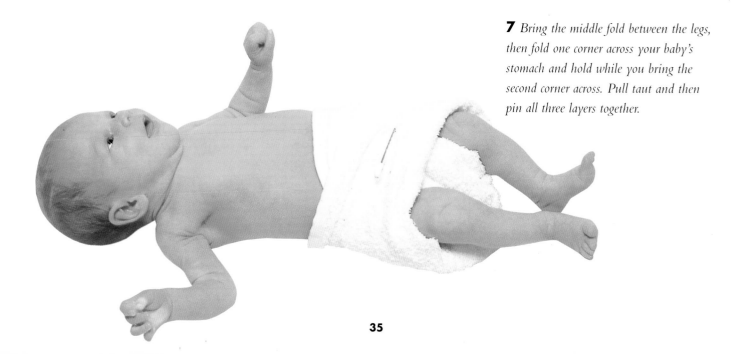

Kite fold

This is suitable from about three months onwards. You can adapt the size of the nappy by varying the depth when you fold the point up, before positioning the liner.

1 *Lay the nappy out flat in front of you so that it is in a diamond shape with one of the corners nearest you.*

2 *Fold the sides into the centre so that you form a kite shape with the nappy.*

5 *Bring the nappy up between the baby's legs and carefully fold one side and then the other into the middle. Secure the nappy with one pin in the centre for a small baby and two pins, one on either side, for a bigger baby.*

wriggling infant cannot roll off if you are changing the nappy on a raised surface.

Remove the soiled nappy. Then clean your baby's bottom thoroughly, wiping away any solid matter with a clean corner of the used nappy, or with a damp tissue or cotton wool soaked in warm water. A baby wipe, or some baby lotion, can be used to finish cleaning the area. Once you have dried your baby's bottom, apply a small amount of a specially formulated barrier cream to protect the skin. Then put on a clean nappy.

WHAT'S IN A NAPPY
You may find the nappy of your new baby is stained dark pink or even

3 *Fold the point at the top down towards the centre so that there is a straight edge along the top.*

4 *Fold the bottom edge up towards the centre, adjusting the fold so that the nappy is the correct size for your baby.*

red. This is because the urine of newborns contains substances called urates. Your newborn's immature bladder cannot hold urine for very long so he may urinate as frequently as 20 times in every 24 hours. This will gradually lessen.

Your baby's first stools will be a blackish-green colour because the meconium from your amniotic fluid is working its way out of his system. Once feeding begins, the stools will change to greenish-brown and then to a yellowish-brown colour. The number of stools passed varies from baby to baby, but generally breast-fed babies pass fewer stools than bottle-fed babies.

DISPOSABLE NAPPIES

There is no doubt that disposables are more convenient than towelling nappies. They are quick and easy to put on and remove and they don't require washing, which is a strong consideration when you think about the extra washing your baby is likely to produce without even including nappies. Their main disadvantages are that they are more expensive than their towelling counterparts and, despite their name, are cumbersome to dispose of. Most end up being wrapped and put in the dustbin; there are special plastic bags that will neutralize strong odours, and these are widely available.

Alternatively, there are a number of portable units available which will wrap and seal the dirty nappy in strong film, so that they can be stored for a number of days and then be disposed of in bulk.

Disposables work by allowing moisture to soak through a top sheet into an absorbent filling, which is protected on the outside by a waterproof backing. They come in a wide range of shapes and sizes and most are also available in boy/girl styles. Most disposables have elasticated legs to ensure a snug fit, and reusable tapes so that you can check whether the nappy needs changing and adjust the leg size. Disposables need to be checked frequently because many of them are so good at keeping your baby dry that you may forget to change them.

TOWELLING NAPPIES

These are a once-only buy which makes them more economical than disposables. Towelling nappies come in a variety of absorbencies and qualities. As a general guide the more absorbent the nappy the more expensive it is, so buy the best you can afford. The nappy can be folded in a number of different ways to fit your baby. It is held together with special pins and covered with reusable plastic pants to prevent leakage. One-way liners can be placed inside the nappy to help keep your baby dry; this method also has the added advantage of allowing you to flush any motions down the lavatory

Putting on a towelling nappy

Towelling nappies can be folded in a variety of ways to suit the age and sex of your child.

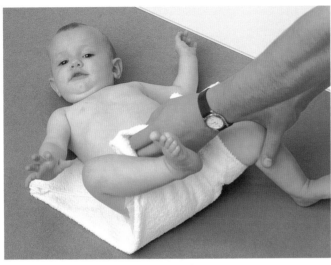

1 *Fold nappy and place a liner in the centre. Lay your baby on the nappy with top edge at waist. Now bring nappy up between her legs.*

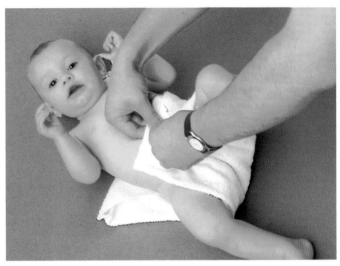

2 *Holding the nappy in place, fold one side over the central panel and secure with a nappy pin.*

3 *Fold the other side into the middle and secure. Always keep your finger between the nappy and your baby's skin when inserting the pin so that there is no risk of pricking your baby.*

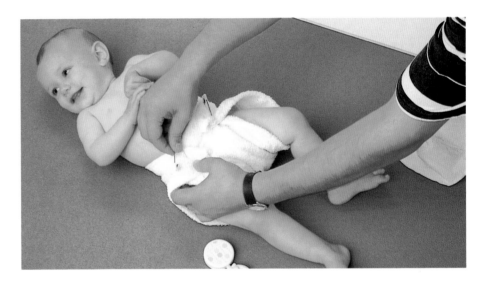

4 *Once the nappy is securely in place you may want to put on a pair of protective plastic pants. Try not to get cross if your baby wets her clean nappy immediately and you have to start all over again.*

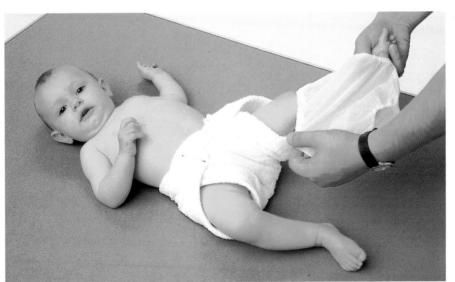

with the minimum of bother.

When working out the price of towelling nappies you need to take into consideration the extra cost of washing powder, the electricity used for washing and drying them, sterilizing solution, plastic pants, nappy liners, and pins. Towelling nappies are harder work than disposables because they need washing, so a washing machine and tumble dryer will make life easier for you. The nappies will need to be sterilized, rinsed, and then well washed and dried. Then they should be aired before being reused.

SHAPED WASHABLE NAPPIES
These wash like towelling nappies but are shaped like disposables with re-sealable fastenings and elasticated legs. They come in various sizes, and have a waterproof backing.

CONVENIENCE AND HELPING THE ENVIRONMENT
The choice of nappy is influenced by environmental considerations. Disposable nappies are a great convenience for busy parents, but there are hidden costs to the environment. Some manufacturers of disposables try to minimize the bulk of their products without cutting down their efficiency. This uses fewer natural resources for materials, but some portion of the nappy still will not break down after being discarded. Towelling nappies would seem environmentally friendlier, but you must assess the cost of energy resources and the impact on the environment of the sterilizers and detergents needed to wash the used nappy.

Whichever type of nappy you choose, you can arrange for services to handle them. You can have disposables delivered regularly for a nominal charge, at a price reduced for bulk ordering. Or, with towelling nappies, you can pay to have the used ones picked up and replaced with clean, sterile ones.

NAPPY RASH
Whichever nappy you choose, it is unlikely that your baby will get through the nappy years without experiencing a nappy rash at some time. The key to avoiding the problem is cleanliness and frequent nappy changes, so that urine and faeces

Putting on a disposable nappy

Disposable nappies are available in a variety of shapes, sizes and absorbencies. Always select the size which is recommended for your baby's weight.

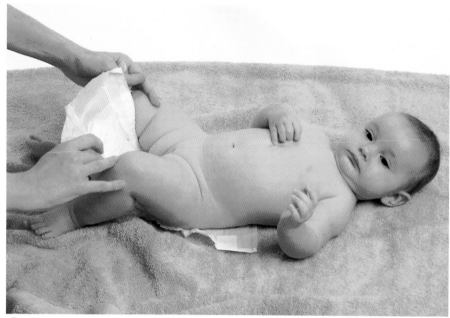

1 *Open out the nappy with the re-sealable tabs at the top. Lay your baby on the nappy so that the top aligns with her waist. Bring the front of the nappy up between her legs.*

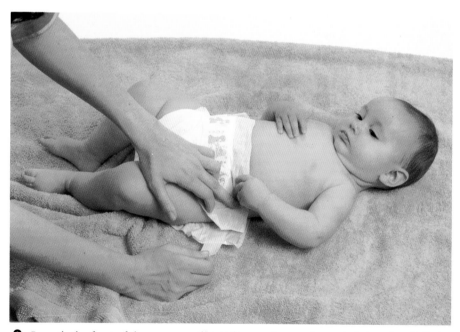

2 *Smooth the front of the nappy so that it fits snugly round your baby's waist. Pull the adhesive tabs firmly towards the front of the nappy and fasten them to secure.*

don't remain in contact with the skin too long. Allow your baby to spend some time naked each day; this will help keep the skin clear.

Nappy rash is sometimes caused by the fungus thrush, and if so an antifungal cream will be needed, so consult your doctor if the rash persists.

DRESSING YOUR BABY

There are clothes to fit every size of newborn, from the tiny premature baby to the bouncing 10-pounder. Most baby clothes are sized by the approximate age and height of the child. Your baby probably won't require a great number of first-size clothes and may well grow into the next size within a matter of weeks – some babies are even big enough when born to go straight into second-size clothes.

Dressing and undressing your newborn can be difficult enough without having to worry about doing up complicated fastenings, so keep first clothes simple and save buttons and bows until later. Choose well-designed baby clothes which allow you to dress and undress your baby with the minimum of fuss. Look for garments which have wide, envelope necks that will stretch, so that you can slip them over baby's head easily. Stretchsuits which have fastenings up the inside leg will allow you to change a nappy without having to remove all your baby's clothes. All-in-one bodysuits, which fasten between the legs, will prevent your baby from getting cold around the middle and are ideal if you dress your baby in separates.

If you have a girl you may well be tempted to put her in dresses from the beginning, but dresses are not practical everyday wear for a young baby. They ride up and can be uncomfortable to lie on, they will allow draughts in around her middle, and they get in the way when she is starting to crawl. It is better to save them for special occasions or for when she's older. Lacy jackets and

shawls are best avoided too, as little fingers can get caught in the holes.

As your baby grows, colourful rompers and dungarees can take the place of stretchsuits. They are versatile and are suitable for both boys and girls. Rompers, which are really stretchsuits without feet, are easy to wear as they allow your baby freedom of movement. When you buy dungarees make sure that they have generous turn-ups and adjustable shoulder straps so that you get the maximum wear out of them.

When the weather is warm, babies need to be dressed in clothes that will keep them comfortably cool, and you should always cover their heads with a sun hat if you are out and about. Outerwear for cold days should be roomy enough to fit easily over everyday clothes.

EASY-CARE FABRICS

Your baby is quite likely to get through as many as three or four changes a day so it makes sense to buy clothes made in easy-care fabrics that will wash and wear well. Check the labels before buying and avoid any garments that are going to need special treatment. Choose natural fabrics as these are best for warmth and absorbency. Pure cotton is ideal for your baby's underwear and also her stretchsuits.

Whether you are machine- or hand-washing garments, always follow the instructions on the labels so that your baby's clothes retain their shape, colour, and texture. Avoid using "biological" washing powders as these may irritate your baby's skin. It is important that all clothes are

well aired and completely dry before being put away.

FOOTWEAR

It is very important that a baby's toes are never restricted by tight footwear. Check regularly that all-in-one-suits, leggings, and tights have enough room in them for the baby to wiggle her toes. Socks, bootees, and tights that have shrunk or been outgrown should be discarded. (The same care should be taken with tight collars, cuffs, mittens and also gloves.)

Your baby will not need proper shoes until she is walking and her feet need protection from the hard ground. If you do put your child in soft shoes before this, these should be made from a lightweight breathable material such as cloth or very soft leather and they must be flexible enough for you to feel her toes through them.

When you come to buy your baby's first shoes always have them fitted at a shop which offers a special fitting service for children. Both your baby's feet should be measured for length and width. If you can afford them, shoes with leather uppers are best. It is essential to check regularly that the shoes still fit and have not become too tight.

For a first layette you will need:
- 3 baby gowns.
- pair of scratch mittens.
- shawl.
- 7 stretchsuits.
- 2 pairs of bootees or socks.
- 4 vests or bodysuits.
- warm outer wear for chilly days.
- sun hat.

How to dress your newborn

Dressing and undressing a newborn can seem difficult at first. Always dress a newborn baby on a flat surface so that you have both hands free.

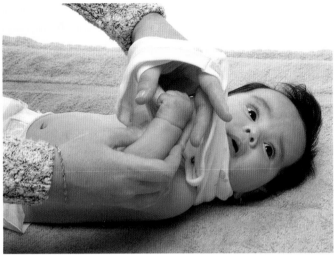

1 *Put the all-in-one vest over your baby's head, raising her head slightly. Then widen one of the arm holes with your hand.*

2 *Using your other hand, gently guide the arm through the sleeve. Repeat with the other arm.*

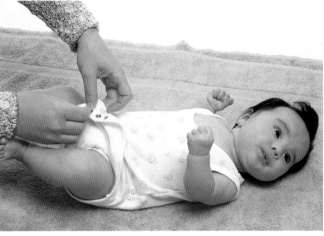

3 *Place your hand under your baby's bottom and pull down the back of the vest.*

4 *Do up the poppers between the legs and make sure that the vest isn't too tight anywhere when fastened.*

5 *Concertina up the leg of the sock and then hold it wide as you ease it over your baby's foot.*

6 *Gently place one foot in the trouser leg and then the other and pull the trousers up.*

7 *Place your hand under your baby's bottom and lift so that you can pull the trousers up over the nappy.*

8 *Adjust the trousers and make sure that the vest is smooth and that there are no puckers that could be uncomfortable to lie on.*

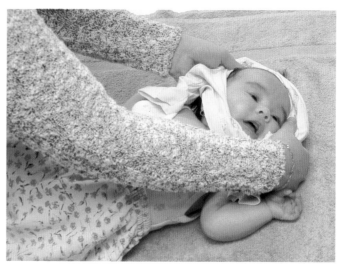

9 *Hold the neck of the T-shirt wide as you slip it over your baby's face and then pull it down over the back of her head.*

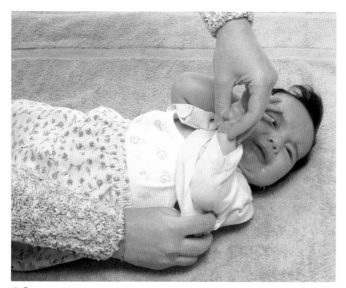

10 *Gently ease your baby's arm through the T-shirt's sleeve and then pull the sleeve down.*

11 *Put her other arm into the sleeve, then pull down top and tuck into her trousers. Your baby is now ready to face the day!*

An all-in-one suit with leg fasteners is ideal for a new baby. The leg opening allows you to change the nappy easily without having to remove any of her clothes.

Rompers and a top are ideal for an older baby and are practical for both boys and girls. The romper straps hold the rompers in place even when your baby is being very active and will help prevent gaps occurring around the middle.

A more mobile baby will be happiest in trousers that will protect her legs as she learns to walk. Make sure the trouser legs clear the floor so that she doesn't trip.

Choose clothes carefully

You will be surprised at how quickly your baby grows during the first 12 months. Select clothes that will mix and match and allow some room for growth. Once she begins to crawl, your baby will need sensible easy-care clothes that will withstand endless washing. Make sure that neck openings are large enough and that garments are easy to unfasten for quick nappy changes. Not all clothes have to be practical; it is nice to buy a couple of special outfits that can be used for parties and days out too.

Dresses look pretty, but are not really practical everyday wear for very young babies or once your baby becomes mobile. Keep dresses for those special occasions.

Rompersuits with short sleeves made in natural fibres are ideal for the summer. Synthetic fibres don't allow the skin to breathe properly and may make your baby feel hot and uncomfortable.

Babies don't need proper shoes until they have started to walk. Soft shoes like these are perfect for little feet in the meantime.

BATHING

When you bath your baby you need to get all you require together before you start. It helps if you can keep all the nappies, pins, pants, and toiletries either in a changing bag or box. A nappy bucket is essential because you'll need somewhere to put the dirty nappy and used cotton wool. A second bucket is also useful for dropping the dirty clothes into as you undress the baby. Any clean clothes and towels should be well aired before you begin and the room where you undress your baby should be warm (a minimum of 21°C/70°F) and draught-free.

When babies are tiny it is easier to bath them in a baby bath on a stand, or one which fits into the big bath.

This way they will be at a comfortable height for you to hold them. Before undressing your baby, fill the bath with warm water, putting the cold in first then the hot, and mix well. Add any bath preparation at this stage. Test that the water is at the right temperature. A special bath thermometer will give you an accurate reading or you can use your elbow.

For bathing you will need:

- Bowl of cooled boiled water, cotton wool and cotton buds (optional) to clean your baby's face before bathing (see topping and tailing).
- Changing mat.
- Bath towel.
- Baby bath preparation.
- Baby shampoo.
- Baby powder.
- Nappy changing equipment and a clean nappy.
- Clean clothes.

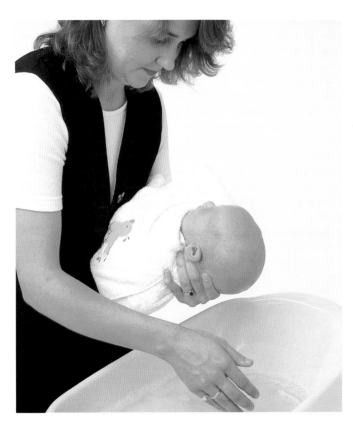

1 *Wrap your baby firmly in a towel. Test the temperature of the bath water again then, having tucked his legs firmly under your arm, hold your baby's head over the bath, supporting his neck and back with your hand.*

2 *Wet his head and apply a mild baby shampoo. Wash the hair with gentle circular movements, keeping the water and shampoo well away from his eyes. Once washed, rinse off the shampoo and lift your baby back onto your knee and towel his hair dry.*

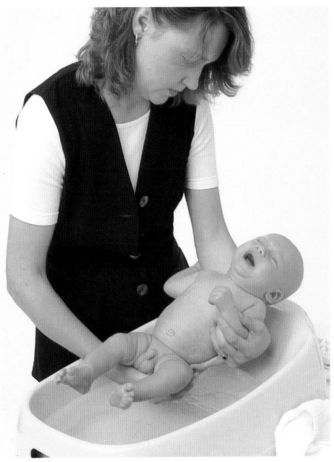

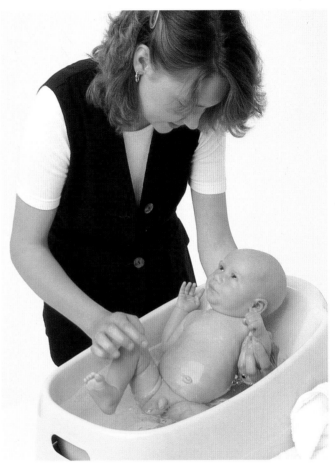

3 *Lift your baby gently into the bath, supporting his head and back on your arm, while holding the arm that is the furthest away from you.*

4 *This leaves your other hand free to wash under his arms and in all the folds and creases. When you have finished, lift your baby out of the bath and into a warm towel.*

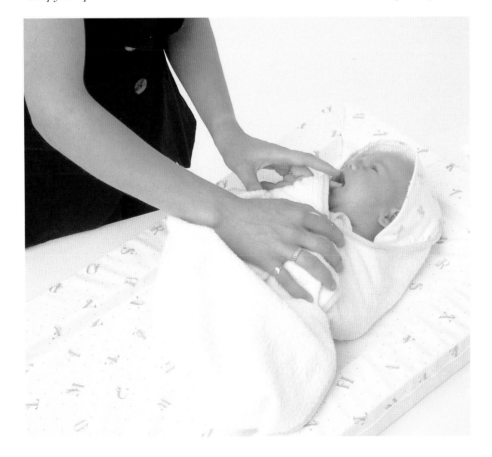

5 *Once you have dried your baby, you may want to apply some baby powder. Put a little powder on your hands and then rub it onto the baby's body, making sure you close the lid tightly after use. Don't sprinkle it on straight from the container in case it gets into your baby's mouth or eyes. It can be dangerous for young infants to inhale powder into their lungs.*

You may find it easier to bath a very young baby in a baby bath. Some of these have their own stand; others, like the one above, fit over a big bath.

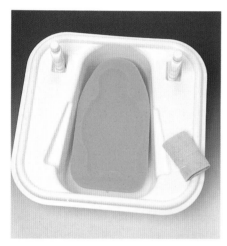

A sponge inlay which fits snugly into the bottom of the bath will prevent your baby from slipping, and will make it easier for you to hold him.

An older baby will be happy to spend time in the bath if he has bath toys to play with. Containers that can be filled and emptied and toys that float and bob about will give hours of fun and entertainment.

Once your baby is old enough to be bathed in the big bath you should cover the taps with a folded towel before putting him in the bath. This will prevent him from accidentally burning himself on the hot tap.

Never leave your baby or toddler alone in the bath. It only takes a few seconds for a child to drown in as little as 5 cm/2 in of water.

• When drying or dressing your baby never leave him unattended on a raised surface. He could easily roll off and hurt himself.

• Always check the temperature of the bath water before putting your baby in the bath.

• If you bath your child in a conventional large bath, place a cover over the taps so that he can't burn himself. A folded towel will do.

• Use a non-slip bath mat in the bath.

• Always put the cold water in first when running the bath.

• If you are using a bath and stand, make sure that it is sturdy and secure before lifting your baby into it.

Above: Your child may enjoy sharing his bath with others, or he may prefer to have a bath alone. If you are intending to bath two or three children together it is often easier to put the smallest into the bath first and then let the others join him one at a time.

Right: Not all children enjoy spending time in the bath. If one child is unhappy about bathtime don't force him to stay in longer than he wants. Always stay in the bathroom with your children so that you can be sure that they are safe.

SLEEPING

Your new baby has no understanding of day and night so during the first weeks of her life she will sleep and wake at random. You may find that she sleeps for 20 hours out of every 24 or for only 12 hours out of 24. Whatever pattern your baby adopts, she will be getting as much sleep as she needs.

Average sleep pattern

Birth	17 hours in every 24	
	Day	**Night**
3 months	5 hours	10 hours
6 months	4 hours	10 hours
9 months	3 hours·	11 hours
12 months	2 hours	11 hours

Your baby's biological clock will dictate when she is ready for sleep in the evenings and this is a good starting point for establishing a regular bedtime. From the very beginning

Try not to let your baby fall asleep before putting him in his cot as he may wake feeling distressed if you are not there.

you should make the hour before bed quiet and relaxing. You may choose this time to give your baby a bath, and you will certainly want to feed and change your baby before putting her down in the cot. You may need to rock or sing to the child until sleep comes, especially if she is very young. During the first three months your baby may sleep better if swaddled in a blanket or sheet – this will prevent tiny limbs from jerking and twitching. These sudden involuntary movements often wake a very young baby. As your child gets older she will begin to settle on her own and you can help by providing things for amusement, such as a mobile and cot toys. Follow the same routine every night so that the

Your baby will enjoy being outside from an early age. Keep her out of direct sun in the shade and have the hood up to protect her from draughts.

baby gradually begins to associate the cot with night-time and sleep.

A baby's room needs to be warm – around 18°C/65°F – so that the child doesn't wake up cold in the

Cot death

All parents are worried about the possibility of cot death, technically known as Sudden Infant Death Syndrome (SIDS). Although the chance of this happening to your baby is remote, it is sensible to take a few simple precautions that are known to reduce the risk.

• Make sure that your baby sleeps either on her back or side, with the lower arm forward to stop the child rolling onto her stomach.

• Keep your baby warm, but not too warm. Check her temperature regularly by feeling the back of her neck or tummy, and use several lightweight blankets so that you can add or take them away to adjust the temperature.

• Don't use a duvet or baby nest because these could be too warm for your baby.

• Do not smoke near your baby and keep her out of a smoky atmosphere.

• If your baby seems unwell, take her to the doctor immediately.

• Try, if you can, to breast feed. It is believed to help reduce the risk of cot death.

• Make sure your baby's room is well ventilated. Leave the door ajar or a window open (but ensure that the baby is not in a draught). Don't leave room heaters on at night. The temperature should be around 18°C/65°F.

• Research is being carried out into the possible link between chemicals found in mattresses and cot death, but as yet no proven link has been found. However, you can safeguard your baby by making sure that her mattress is kept clean, dry and well aired.

Bedtime tips

• Encourage your baby to sleep while there are background noises going on. This way she won't expect silence at bedtime.

• Put a selection of toys in the cot to provide amusement if she wakes early.

• Make night feeds as quick and quiet as possible, keeping the lights low and changing the baby first. Don't do anything stimulating.

• Put the baby down to sleep in the cot at night so that she comes to associate it with sleep.

• Wrap up a newborn baby firmly so that she feels secure.

An older baby will enjoy looking at a mobile when he is awake in his cot.

the day. Stimulate your baby by talking and playing with her in the daytime when she is awake. Keep feeding and changing down to a minimum amount of time during the night so that your baby learns that this is not a time for being sociable.

Above: If your baby prefers to sleep on her side, make sure her lower arm is in a forward position to stop her rolling onto her stomach.

Below: Check your baby's body warmth regularly at night, and remove some blankets if she feels too warm.

night. Put your baby down to sleep in a vest, nappy, and stretchsuit and cover her with a sheet and several layers of blankets. You can check for body warmth during the night by feeling the tummy or the back of the neck, then you can add or take away blankets accordingly. If your baby seems worried by the dark, leave a nightlight on near the cot.

You can help your infant develop a better sleeping pattern by encouraging her to be more awake during

CRYING

Your response to your child's crying and the way you comfort him can influence the bond that grows between you. There is no risk of spoiling your child by responding to his cries. It is impossible to give a young baby too much love. By going to your baby you will be showing him that you care and this in turn will help to form a deep, loving relationship between you.

WHY BABIES CRY

Babies cry for a lot of different reasons and you need to understand what makes your baby cry so that you can provide comfort. Your newborn may cry a lot because this is the main means of communicating with you. The infant needs to be able to let you know that the world he is now in is a strange and sometimes frightening place. Once he has adapted to the new environment and you have developed a routine that takes account of his likes and dislikes,

the amount of crying will gradually start to decrease.

Hunger is the most common cause of crying and you will soon learn to recognize when your baby is hungry. The first action is to feed on demand – a very young baby may need feeding about every two or three hours.

Being too hot or too cold can also make a baby cry. A young baby can't regulate his own temperature and he can easily become too hot or too cold, so it is important to keep a check on an infant's temperature. You should make sure that your baby's room is kept at a constant 18°C/65°F. Wet or dirty nappies do not cause crying except when the wet nappy gets cold.

Your new baby will probably hate being undressed, even in a warm room. This is because the feel of clothing on the skin creates a secure feeling, so when it is removed the infant cries. Keep undressing to a

Crying cures

- Movement soothes a baby so try rocking him or walking around holding him on your shoulder.
- Put your baby in a bouncing seat that will move very gently.
- Push him backwards and forwards in the pram.
- Put the baby in his car seat and go for a drive.
- Talk, sing, or croon soothingly.
- Put on the radio or TV or turn on the vacuum cleaner.
- Distract the baby with a noisy toy.
- Play a tape of calm music.
- Carry a young baby next to your body in a sling.

minimum in the first few weeks. Top and tail rather than bath your baby so that you only need to remove a bit of clothing at a time. When you do undress him completely, wrap him in a towel to give him a feeling of security.

Pain is a definite cause of crying, but it may be hard for you to locate the cause of the actual pain. If you

Not being allowed to do what he wants, when he wants, can lead to a child's tears of frustration.

Waiting for a bottle to cool down can be tiresome and can lead to angry tears from a hungry baby.

can, remove the source of the pain –
for example an open nappy pin. If
you can't find a reason for the pain,
don't just leave your baby to cry;
pick him up and comfort him. Stay
with your baby until he is completely calm. If your baby seems feverish
or just generally unwell, always seek
medical advice.

Any baby will normally start crying when he is tired. If you think
that this is the cause, put your child
down to sleep in a dimly lit, warm
room. If necessary, rock or sing a
soothing song to him until he has
completely calmed down and starts
to become sleepy.

Tiredness is a common reason for tears before bedtime.

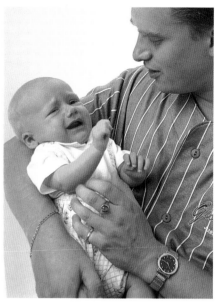

The discomfort of wind after a feed can cause a baby's tears.

Sometimes it all gets too much for a young child and the only way to show his feelings is to scream.

COLIC

Young babies sometimes have prolonged periods of crying during the day which are frequently attributed to colic. These crying spells often take place around the time of the evening feed, although they can happen at any time of day. Colic, if it is going to occur, usually starts within the first three weeks after birth and normally lasts until around three months, although it can go on for longer. It generally stops as abruptly as it starts, having caused your baby no harm.

Although no one knows exactly what colic is, or what causes it, many doctors believe that it is a type of stomach ache that occurs in spasms, and makes the baby draw up her legs in pain. The pattern of crying would indicate cramp-like pains; the baby is miserable and distressed, then calms down for a few minutes before starting to scream again. This may continue for several hours at a time, which can become very wearing and upsetting for both of you.

POSSIBLE CAUSES

Colic has been blamed on many things and it is certainly worth investigating all the possibilities if your baby suffers from it. Since colic affects both bottle- and breast-fed babies the method of feeding is not thought to be the cause. However, if you are breast-feeding it could be something that you are eating which is causing the problem. Try cutting out of your diet anything you have eaten during the previous 24 hours which you think might have affected your baby. It has been suggested that the amount of feeds offered – both too little and too much – could be to blame, or that the milk, if bottle-feeding, could be too hot or too cold, or the feeds too weak or too rich. Remember, when you make up bottle feeds it is essential to follow the manufacturer's instructions.

Other possible causes are constipation, diarrhoea, indigestion or intestinal cramps. Vigorously crying babies are almost always healthy, but if your baby looks pale or ill, seek medical advice.

There may also be a link between tension and colic, which can lead to a chain reaction. The end of the day is usually a busy time in a household and you may be tired and tense as you try to prepare the baby for bed, tidy up, and get a meal ready. Your baby is sensitive to your moods and may respond to tension by crying which, of course, increases your anxiety, with the result that the crying becomes prolonged and ends when you are both exhausted.

WHAT TO DO

There is no reliable treatment for colic and, although there are some over-the-counter medicines available you should always consult your doctor before giving them to your baby. On a practical level you can rearrange your day by preparing the evening meal earlier, so that you have time to spend comforting your baby during this crying period. Although there is little you can do to ease your baby's discomfort completely, holding him against you, so that there is gentle pressure and warmth on her stomach, and rubbing her back soothingly may be of some help. Try to share the comforting with your partner to spread the strain, and remember that colic doesn't last for more than a few months so, although it is awful at the time, it will not last for ever.

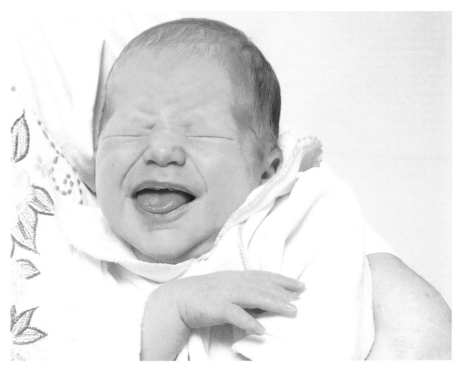

Colic can start as early as three weeks and may last until your baby is three months old. Be patient; it will pass and it won't do your baby any harm.

TEETH

At around six months your baby's milk teeth will start to emerge and by the age of two-and-a-half all 20 first teeth will usually have appeared. Every tooth has two parts: the crown, which can be seen in the mouth; and the root, which anchors

Your baby's first teeth will start to emerge at around six months old, and you should start to clean them as soon as they appear in the gums.

the tooth to the jaw. The outside of the tooth is made of enamel which protects the crown and provides a strong surface for chewing. Because the enamel is not fully formed when the teeth first come through, calcium and other minerals are required over the next six to 12 months to strengthen it. These minerals are found in the saliva and plaque in your child's mouth and, under normal conditions, will steadily accumulate in the teeth. But calcium and phosphates in the enamel frequently come under attack from acids that are formed by the bacteria living in plaque. These bacteria use carbohydrates, such as sugar, to generate the acid.

Your baby needs carbohydrates, but food and drink containing a lot of simple sugars such as sucrose, fructose, and glucose will speed up the production of the acids which can damage

When he is teething your child will chew anything, even his fingers. Try offering her finger foods, such as a stick of raw carrot, as something different to chew on.

teeth. It is not just the amount of sugar she eats that affects your child's teeth, it is also the frequency of her consumption of sugary food and drink. Drinks taken slowly, or sugary foods eaten over a long period of time, keep the sugar content of the

Chewing and biting on things is often one of the first signs of teething in a baby, and this may occur some weeks before any teeth appear.

Before you start trying to brush your baby's teeth, it is a good idea to let him play with his toothbrush so that he becomes familiar with it and does not cause a fuss when you put it in his mouth.

Your child will find it good fun attempting to brush his own teeth from a very early age.

You will need to clean your child's teeth until he is old enough to do it himself. A fluoride toothpaste will help protect his teeth and gums.

mouth high, which means that calcium and phosphates are being removed for longer and less time is available to replace them. Generally, the lower the sugar content of food and drink the better they are for the teeth because it is the total sugar levels, not just added sugar, that counts. This is why you should never add sugar to your baby's food or drinks and you should always dilute concentrated drinks and give them in a trainer cup rather than a feeding bottle.

CLEANING TEETH

As soon as your baby's first teeth appear, you should clean them every morning and night. Cleaning the teeth at night, before bed, is especially important because the flow of protective saliva decreases when your baby is asleep, which means that any sugar in the mouth allows the plaque to stay acidic for a prolonged period.

In the morning, brushing your baby's teeth will help to remove any build-up of plaque that has occurred during the night.

The main point of cleaning teeth is to remove as much plaque as possible, and toothpaste does this with the aid of abrasives; there are toothpastes specially formulated to be suitable for young children. A pea-sized amount of toothpaste on the brush is all that is required to clean a mouth full of teeth. You'll probably find it easiest at first to use your finger wrapped in a soft cloth and then, when your baby has got used to the idea of having his teeth cleaned, you can start to clean his teeth with a soft baby toothbrush.

Since the introduction of fluoride toothpastes, children's teeth have been healthier. Fluoride, which is present in most toothpastes, works by making the enamel stronger

As your child starts to get teeth she will experiment with the chewing action on her favourite toys.

against attack from plaque. The amount of fluoride children should use varies according to their age and the fluoride levels already present in the water.

THE DENTIST

Take your baby with you when you go for your own dental check-ups so that he will become familiar with the dentist and the surgery. By getting your child used to having his teeth inspected before he needs treatment, he will then experience no alarm at the thought of going to the dentist. A child usually won't need to have an actual dental check-up until he is about three years of age, when your dentist will check to see that the teeth are developing properly. The dentist will also be able to advise you about any special protective treatments available for your child.

Cleaning your young baby's new teeth at bedtime is essential to prevent the build-up of plaque as he sleeps.

IMMUNIZATION

Diseases such as measles, mumps, whooping cough, rubella (German measles), diphtheria, tetanus, polio, and Haemophilus influenzae type b (a cause of meningitis) can be very serious and, in very young children, can be fatal. Immunization offers long-lasting protection against these diseases. If you are concerned about your child having the immunizations, or are worried about allergic reactions, or because there is a family history of convulsions, don't just decide not to have your child immunized, discuss it with your doctor.

The triple vaccine or DPT, which immunizes against diphtheria, whooping cough (the P in DPT stands for Pertussis – the medical name for whooping cough) and tetanus, is usually given as one injection at two months, three months, and four months of age. Hib vaccine, which immunizes against Haemophilus influenzae type b, the most common bacterial meningitis in the under-fives, is given by injection at the same time as DPT. Polio vaccine is given by mouth in three doses also at the same time as the DPT injections. With all of these it is important to complete the course of three doses to ensure the maximum immunity. MMR immunizes against measles, mumps, and rubella and is given in one injection – normally between 12 and 15 months.

Your newborn baby may also be offered immunization against tuberculosis (TB) with a BCG vaccine if you are in or from a high-risk area, or if you come from a family that has a history of TB.

SIDE-EFFECTS

Many parents worry about possible side-effects of these vaccines, especially from the whooping cough vaccine and MMR. However, research shows that the risk of harmful complications from any of the vaccines on the schedule is extremely small. In fact, a child is much more at risk from the diseases themselves than from immunization.

After any immunization your child may feel a bit off-colour for a while and may even run a slight temperature. It is quite normal for the skin around the site of the injection to become red and sore or slightly swollen. But if you are at all worried about your child you should contact your doctor.

Any side-effects from the triple vaccine are usually mild. Your baby may be slightly feverish and appear unhappy for up to 24 hours after the injection. Very occasionally a convulsion occurs as a result of the fever, but this is over very quickly and has no lasting effect. The whooping cough part of this vaccination is the one that most parents worry about, but the latest research suggests that there is no proven link between the vaccine and brain damage. The Hib vaccination has similar side-effects to

the triple vaccine: some redness and swelling at the injection site and slight fever and irritability.

The MMR immunization has no immediate side-effect, although some children develop a mild fever and rash seven to ten days after the injection, others sometimes get a very mild form of mumps. If either of these reactions occur they are not infectious. In rare cases, a child may have an extreme reaction to the vaccine, such as a convulsion with fever or encephalitis (inflammation of the brain). But the vaccine that was associated with this reaction has now been replaced.

If your baby is feverish or acutely unwell or has had a severe reaction to an earlier immunization, you should not have her immunized again without talking first to your doctor. Always remember to tell the doctor who is doing the immunization if your baby is taking medication or if she has a severe allergic reaction to eggs. If the baby is vomiting or has diarrhoea it is better to put off giving the polio vaccine until she is better.

THE DISEASES

Immunizations have developed over the years and many diseases which were formerly feared are no longer threats. This is the result of a sound immunization programme applied to virtually all children. Often parents

At 2 months:	
Diphtheria	}
Whooping cough	}DPT one injection
Tetanus	}
Hib	}one injection
Polio	}by mouth

At 3 months:	
Diphtheria	}
Whooping cough	}DPT one injection
Tetanus	}
Hib	}one injection
Polio	}by mouth

are vague about the actual disease themselves, so it is worth familiarizing yourself with the conditions and their symptoms:

Diphtheria starts with a sore throat and then quickly develops into a serious illness which blocks the nose and throat, making it difficult and sometimes nearly impossible for a child to breathe. It can last for weeks and can often be fatal.

Tetanus is caused by germs from dirt or soil getting into an open wound or burn. It attacks the nervous system causing painful muscle spasms. Immunization has made it rare, but there is still a real chance of getting it and it can be fatal.

Whooping cough is a highly infectious disease which causes long bouts of coughing and choking, leaving the sufferer exhausted. These bouts can occur up to 50 times in one day and the cough can last two to three months. Whooping cough can cause convulsions, ear infections, pneumonia, bronchitis, and even brain damage. It can prove fatal, especially in children who are under one year of age.

Haemophilus influenzae type b is the commonest form of bacterial meningitis in the under-fives. It causes epiglottitis (a severe form of croup), pneumonia, blood poisoning, and infections of the bones and joints. It affects babies under a year most severely and can be fatal.

Polio attacks the nervous system and causes muscle paralysis. If it affects the breathing the sufferer will need help to breathe and could even die. Thankfully, polio is extremely rare in most western countries because of immunization, but there is still a risk of contact with the disease through foreign travel, which is why immunization is still important. Adults should check to see if they need a polio booster when they take their baby for immunization.

Measles can be much more serious than people think because it is the disease most likely to cause encephalitis (inflammation of the brain). It begins like a bad cold with a fever and then a rash appears which is often accompanied by a bad cough and high temperature. Measles can cause convulsions, ear infections, bronchitis, and pneumonia; it can sometimes be fatal.

Mumps is usually a mild illness, but it can have serious complications which affect both boys and girls, and it can cause permanent deafness.

Rubella (German measles) is a mild disease, but one which can harm an unborn baby if a woman catches it when she is pregnant. The risk is particularly high during the first four months of pregnancy. Babies whose mothers get rubella during pregnancy can be born deaf, blind, and with heart and brain damage.

Tuberculosis (TB) usually affects

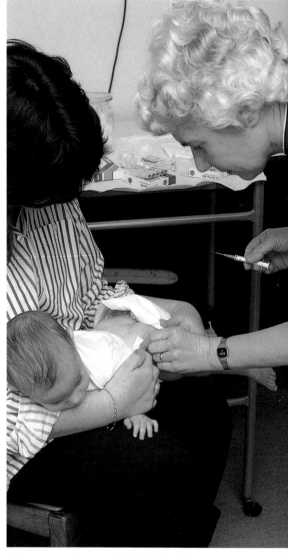

At two months your child will be given his first immunizations. Although they will probably cause some momentary discomfort it will all soon be forgotten with a cuddle.

the lungs; symptoms include a cough, fever, or night sweats. Children are vulnerable and develop TB meningitis more often than adults.

Immunization timetable

At 4 months:		At 12-15 months:		At 3-5 years (pre-school booster):	
Diphtheria	}	Measles	}	Diphtheria	}one booster
Whooping cough	}DPT one injection	Mumps	}MMR one injection	Tetanus	}injection
Tetanus	}	Rubella	}	Polio	}by mouth
Hib	}one injection				
Polio	}by mouth				

CHILDHOOD ILLNESSES

Knowing what to do when your child is ill and when you should call the doctor is something that comes with experience. Common symptoms that indicate that your child is unwell include sickness, diarrhoea, or a high temperature. These may be accompanied by unusual behaviour such as listlessness, refusing to eat, and crying for no apparent reason. However, it is not always easy to tell when a very young baby is unwell so you should trust your instincts – you know your baby better than anyone. Signs indicating that a baby is ill and that you should call the doctor include refusing feeds, a fit or convulsion, extreme drowsiness, difficulty in breathing, severe diarrhoea, vomiting, high fever and the appearance of unusual rashes.

DEALING WITH ILLNESS

Fever occurs when the body temperature rises above normal and is usually caused by an infection. If your child is feverish he will need a lot of cold fluids to drink and a dose of paracetamol syrup to bring his temperature down (aspirin should not be given to children under the age of 12, unless specifically prescribed by your doctor).

If your child is very feverish, keep him in bed and cool him down. This can be done by sponging him all over with tepid water, then covering him with a light sheet and making sure that he drinks plenty of liquids. Alternatively, put a cool fan next to the bed – but safely out of reach.

The easiest way of detecting feverish illness is by taking your child's temperature. This can be done by using a clinical thermometer which is placed under your baby's arm, or in the groin – older children can hold it under their tongue. Alternatively, you can hold a fever strip on your child's forehead. Whichever method you use, make sure that you start with a low reading. A clinical thermometer should have the mercury shaken down close to the bulb. A normal temperature is 37°C/98.6°F, but a child's can vary between 36°C/96.8°F and 37.5°C/99.5°F. You must phone your doctor if the temperature goes over 39°C/102°F, or if it remains above normal for more than two days.

Medicines for young children usually come in liquid form and can be given to them by dropper, or by using a specially designed spoon; older children can manage with an ordinary spoon. It is important that you know what the medicine is, what it does, and the correct dosage before you give it to your child. If you are in any doubt, check the details with your pharmacist.

You are the best person to judge whether your child is unwell as you know him better than anyone else. As you become more experienced as a parent you will know whether you need to call the doctor. If you are unsure, it is always better to seek medical advice.

It may be easier to take a young baby's temperature using a fever strip. Place the strip on your child's forehead and hold it there for 15–20 seconds to get the necessary reading.

A more accurate way of taking a temperature is with a clinical thermometer. Place it under your child's arm, in the armpit, and hold it in position for two or three minutes.

SPECIFIC CONDITIONS:
COUGHS AND COLDS

Colds are caused by air-borne viruses, not bacteria, so antibiotics can't be used to help relieve the symptoms. If your child is suffering from a blocked or runny nose, you may need to buy a nasal decongestant or your doctor may prescribe some nose drops, particularly if the cold is hindering your baby's feeding. Always seek advice from your doctor or health visitor if a cold is affecting your child's breathing. It is better to be safe than sorry.

Irritating coughs often occur with a cold so if your child has a dry cough ask your pharmacist to recommend a soothing linctus that is suitable for children.

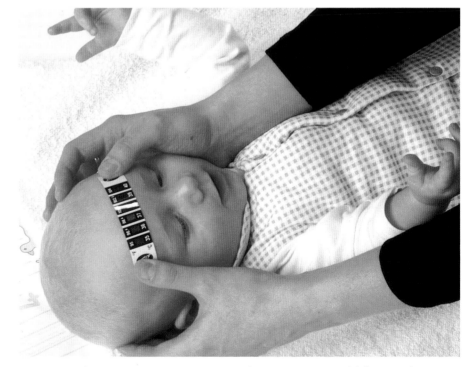

Although a fever strip is not as accurate as a thermometer it is useful for a quick assessment. It will show a raised temperature so that you can take the appropriate action.

Medicines for young children usually come in liquid form and can be given on a tea-spoon. Sit your baby on your knee and hold his hands out of the way as you spoon the medicine into his mouth.

If your child appears hot and feverish you can help to cool him down by wiping his forehead with a face cloth that has been wrung out in cold water.

EAR INFECTIONS

Problems with a child's ears often accompany a cold. One of the first signs is if your baby starts pulling at one of his ears, which might appear red, but he may also just cry a lot and seem generally unwell. Paracetamol syrup will help relieve the pain, but an antibiotic may also be required to clear up any infection, so you will need to consult your doctor for advice. Do not take your child swimming with an ear infection.

CONSTIPATION AND DIARRHOEA

If a child is having difficulty passing stools because they are hard, the problem is most likely to be constipation. A change in diet will be necessary. Including more water, fruit, vegetables, and fibre will help solve the problem. If the problem still continues to persist, a mild laxative may be required. Consult your health visitor for advice.

Diarrhoea is the frequent passing of loose, watery stools. If a baby is being bottle-fed or being weaned, you should omit one or two milk feeds and solids and offer plenty of clear fluids instead, including an oral rehydration mixture if the loose stools continue. Breast-fed babies can continue their milk feeds as normal.

You should contact your doctor if the diarrhoea persists after a period of 12 hours, or if it is accompanied by vomiting because the baby could become dehydrated.

TEETHING

The first signs of teething in a young child are often a red area on his cheek, excessive dribbling, and he starts chewing on his fingers. A teething gel, containing a local anaesthetic, will help to give some relief, but you will need to watch out for any sign of allergic reactions to the gel. These can include a noticeable reddening or swelling of the gums.

VOMITING

If your baby starts to vomit frequently or violently, and if there is any other sign of illness, you should always contact your doctor immediately as young babies can very quickly become dehydrated if they are sick.

Older children can be sick once or twice without suffering any lasting effect. Give your child plenty of clear fluids to drink and don't bother about trying to offer him any tempting food until he is feeling better.

CHILDHOOD DISEASES

There are a number of diseases that affect most children. If treated promptly, they pose no serious threat and will probably give immunity to the sufferer. The key thing for the parent is to recognize the condition as close to its onset as possible and take the appropriate action.

GERMAN MEASLES (RUBELLA)

This is usually a mild illness which causes few problems. It is rare for a child to get German measles in the first six months if the mother has had the infection or has been immunized. The incubation period is 10-21 days and the virus is spread through the coughing and sneezing of an infected person. It is infectious from the day before the rash appears and for two days after its appearance. It is very important to keep your child away from any woman who might be pregnant if you suspect German measles because it can seriously damage an unborn baby.

Symptoms: The first sign is usually a rash that starts on the face and then spreads to the trunk. The spots are pink, pinpoint in size, separate (not blotchy), and are not raised above the level of the skin. The rash is not

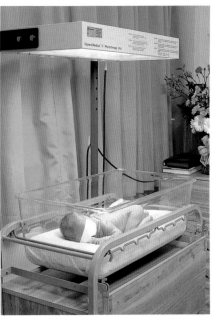

Some babies are born with slight jaundice, a yellowing of the skin, which may need treatment with ultra-violet light. It is usually carried out in the post-natal ward.

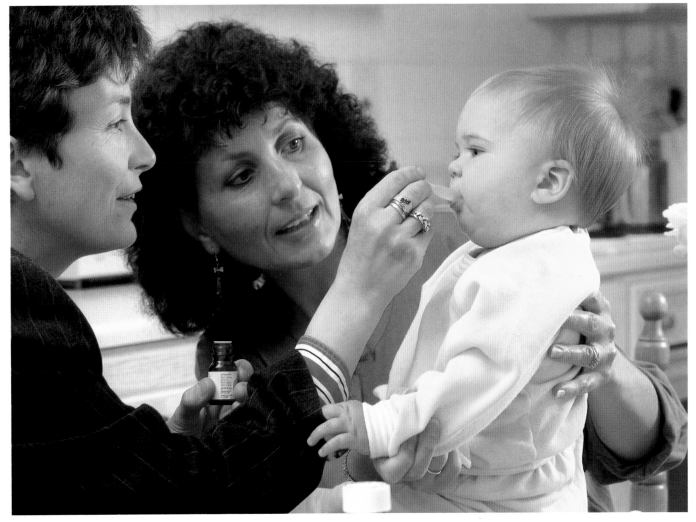

The polio vaccine will probably be given to your baby on a spoon at the same time as he has his other injections.

itchy and lasts for only two or three days. It may be accompanied by a slightly runny nose and a little redness around the eyes and swollen glands in the neck, the back of the head, and behind the ears. These may remain swollen for a few days.

Treatment: Check your child's temperature at least twice a day and give plenty of fluids if the temperature is at all raised.

Call the doctor: If you think your child has German measles, contact your doctor to confirm it. Do not take your child to the surgery because of possible contact with a pregnant woman.

MEASLES

It is rare for a child under six months to get measles if the mother had measles as a child, because the mother's immunity is passed on to the baby. The incubation period is 10-15 days and your child is infectious about six days before the rash appears and for five days afterwards. The virus is spread through droplets from the nose and throat of an infected person.

Symptoms: The first symptoms are a slightly raised temperature, runny

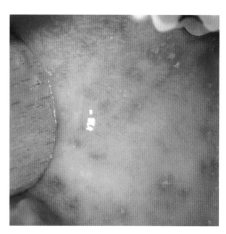

One of the first signs of measles are Koplik's spots which appear inside a child's cheeks. The spots are small and red and have a white centre.

nose, cough, redness of the eyes, lethargy, and loss of appetite. Two or three days later white spots about the size of a pinhead, with a surrounding red area, can be seen on the inside of the cheeks. These last for a few days then a blotchy, slightly raised, red rash appears behind the ears and on the face and then spreads to the chest during the next 24 hours. By the third and fourth day it will have spread over the arms and legs and will have reached the feet. The rash is not itchy but it will be accompanied by a high temperature. As the rash fades so the temperature falls.

Treatment: Bring the fever down. If your child's eyes become crusted, wipe them gently with cotton wool dipped in cooled boiled water. Your child can get out of bed as soon as she is feeling better.

Call the doctor: If your child is no better three days after the rash develops; if the child's temperature rises very rapidly; if earache or breathing difficulties develop.

MUMPS

This affects the glands in the neck and in front of the ears and causes swelling. Sometimes mumps causes inflammation of the testicles, but this is rare in boys before puberty. Mumps is unlikely to affect a baby under the age of six months. The incubation period is 12-21 days. Mumps is spread by droplet infection and it is infectious from two days before the swelling appears and until it disappears.

Symptoms: Pain and swelling in one or both of the parotid glands which are situated just in front of the ears. The swelling makes the face appear puffy and reaches its maximum in about two days. It subsides within about five days.

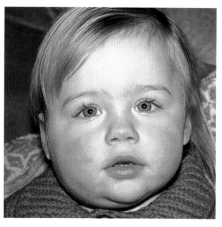

With mumps, your child's face will become swollen and he may find it hard to swallow. Make sure he drinks plenty of liquids and give him jelly and ice cream to eat.

Treatment: Give a suitable painkiller to reduce discomfort. Give your child easy-to-swallow foods such as ice cream and jelly and plenty of liquids, but avoid acidic drinks. If opening the mouth is painful, try getting her to drink through a straw. Warmth will help to soothe the swelling, so heat a soft cloth and hold it gently to her cheeks.

Call the doctor: If your child develops bad pains in her stomach or, if a boy, has a red testicle. Your doctor should be told if you suspect that your child has mumps.

WHOOPING COUGH

This can occur at any age and is one of the most serious common infectious diseases. The incubation period is 7-10 days and the germ is spread through droplet infection. A child is infectious from about two days before the onset of the cough until about three weeks later.

Symptoms: Whooping cough starts with a slight cough and sneezing and is often mistaken for an ordinary cold. It develops into severe bouts of 10-20 short, dry coughs which occur during the day and night – these are often worse during the night. In children over 18 months of age a long attack of coughing is followed by a sharp intake of breath which may produce the crowing or whooping sound. Not all children develop the whoop. During bad bouts of coughing your child may vomit, become red in the face and sweat. The cough can last for two to three months.

Treatment: Stay with the child during her coughing fits because they are distressing and she will need you to comfort her. Try lying her face-down across your lap while she coughs. Sleep with her at night when the cough is at its worst. Keep a bowl near her in case of vomiting and clean it afterwards with disinfectant so that the infection isn't spread. Try to keep your child entertained to distract her from coughing.

Call the doctor: Immediately if you suspect that your child has whooping cough. The doctor may prescribe a cough suppressant and an antibiotic. A very young baby may need to be admitted to hospital if the coughing is affecting breathing.

CHICKENPOX

This is a highly infectious but usually mild disease in childhood (it can be serious if it occurs during adulthood). It is caused by one of the herpes group of viruses and is transmitted through direct contact with an infected person. The incubation period is 14-21 days and it is most infectious before the rash appears, which makes it difficult to isolate an infected child from others.

Symptoms: Chickenpox often starts with a fever, which may be accompanied by a headache and is then followed by a rash. Sometimes the only sign is the rash, which appears mainly on the trunk and

then spreads to the rest of the body and may even occur in the mouth. The rash consists of small red spots that quickly turn into itchy blisters. These gradually dry to form crusts which can remain for a few weeks. New spots appear in batches so an area may be covered in both crusty spots and new blisters. Scars only occur if the spots are scratched or if they become infected. Your child is infectious to other children until new blisters have stopped appearing,

which normally takes about one week.

Treatment: Treat any fever as previously described. Keep your child's nails very short to prevent her from scratching and infecting the spots. Apply calamine lotion to help reduce the itchiness. A handful of bicarbonate of soda added to a cool bath will also ease itchiness.

Call the doctor: If the itchiness is really causing a serious problem or if any of the spots have become infected or are very painful.

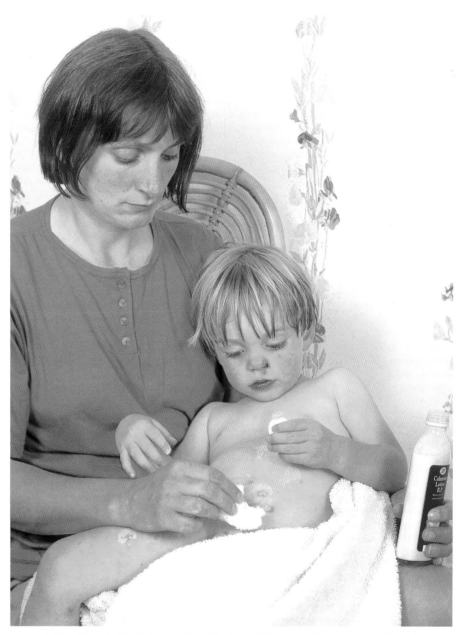

Your child will probably feel miserable if he has chickenpox. Try to prevent him from scratching the spots as this will lead to scarring. Applying some calamine lotion to the spots will help reduce the itchiness and irritation.

PLAY

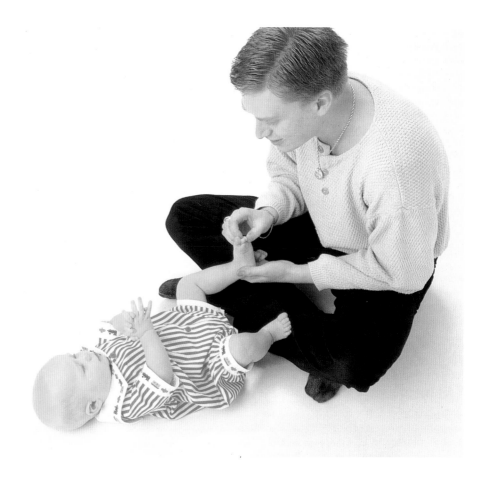

Introduce your baby to games by teaching him nursery rhymes like "this little piggy went to market".

A baby is born with the potential to learn and play. She can see, hear, and feel. She is aware of her environment and will respond from birth to brightly coloured, moving objects and to sounds. She learns all the time and play is one of the ways in which she develops new skills, while toys are the play tools that she uses to stimulate herself at each stage of development. Toys don't have to be elaborate; your child will invent her own games and use everyday objects as toys when she is young. Watching you and trying to imitate your voice and facial expressions will provide hours of entertainment in the early months. Ultimately, the toy that a child enjoys and plays with most will give her the greatest learning experience, and in the first weeks of life this "toy" will be you.

Your child will change very rapidly during the first year so that a toy that entertains her at two months will not appeal to her when she is a year old. As she develops, your child will need different stimuli and the choice of toys for each stage of development should reflect these different needs. It is also very important that the toys you give a child are appropriate to this age. A toy designed for a younger child will be boring, while a toy for an older child may be too complicated and may even be dangerous if it contains small pieces on which a young baby could choke.

BIRTH TO THREE MONTHS

During the first few months, your baby is developing her basic senses – touch, sight, and sound. She needs

Your child will be fascinated by nursery rhymes that involve actions that use his hands.

Because the end of "round and round the garden" includes tickling your baby, he will associate it with fun and ask for more.

As your child develops she will start to enjoy playing games with you such as "peek-a-boo"

As you teach her the game, she will enjoy "hiding" behind the chair and peeking out at you from behind the legs.

Games to play

• Gently bounce your baby up and down on your knee in rhythm to a nursery rhyme.

• Hold her palm open and play "round and round the garden" ending up with a tickle under her arm.

• Use her toes to play "this little piggy went to market".

• Take your baby as your partner and dance around the room with her in your arms.

You can buy your baby many expensive toys, but she'll still enjoy playing with simple kitchen utensils. Always make sure they have no sharp edges.

toys which will stimulate these senses and give experience of colours, textures, materials, and shapes. A good first toy is a mobile, hung where your baby can study it at leisure. It doesn't have to be expensive – one made from pictures cut from a magazine and suspended from a coat hanger will be just as effective as one you buy. Once your baby begins to wave her hands around and tries to swipe at things, she will enjoy toys that make a noise or that react to her actions, a rattle for example. This will give your child a sense of control as well as encouraging the development of manual skills and hand and eye co-ordination.

A newborn baby's hands are usually held closed in fists, but she will gradually relax them so that if you place an object in her open palm she will close her hand around it for a few seconds. The strong grasp reflex she was born with will have disappeared so that she will probably drop the object within a few seconds. By the

An activity centre is ideal for babies around nine months as they will love to push the buttons and manipulate all the different shapes and knobs.

age of two or three months she will try reaching out to touch things. These first grasping movements are important steps towards learning hand-eye co-ordination.

Once your baby is old enough to sit in a bouncing cradle she will be able to see more of the world around her and her hands will be free to explore. A toy fastened across the front of the cradle will encourage her to bring her hands forward to try and hit it to make it move. Once she has done this, she will want to do it again and again; gradually she sees that she is responsible for making this happen and her movements become more deliberate.

A newborn is acutely aware of sounds and will already have become familiar with your voice while in the womb. Talking and singing to your baby from the time she is born will encourage her to listen and help her develop her own speech later. As she gets older, hold her on your lap and try having a conversation with her. Say something, then wait until your baby makes a noise in response. Her response will be slow at first so allow her plenty of time. These conversations will help her learn about taking turns, listening, and copying – all essential parts of communication. Once your baby has got used to life

As she starts to move around, your baby will get pleasure from pushing a baby walker. She will also enjoy trying to put plastic shapes in the right holes on the walker.

outside the womb, she will find touch and the freedom to move her limbs exciting. Different textures will give her new sensations of touch, so offer her various things to feel that will give her experience of rough, soft, silky, or smooth textures. Bathing and changing times will provide an opportunity for your baby to explore touch and sensation. She will like the feeling of not being hampered by nappies and clothing and should enjoy the sensation of warm water next to her skin. Try tickling her gently, blowing raspberries on her abdomen, and kissing her toes when she is undressed.

THREE TO SIX MONTHS

As your baby grows and her movements become more controlled, she will reach out for things and take them in her hands. Her grip becomes stronger and she will be able to hold a wider variety of items. This means that she will start to experience the difference between things that are light and heavy, soft and hard. Her curiosity will be endless and every object will be a plaything. She may prefer to use her mouth rather than her hands to explore things at this age, so it is important to make sure that she can't get hold of anything which could do her any harm.

Your baby will probably play happily for short periods on her own, but she needs you to encourage her. When you play with your baby get her to do things for herself; allow her to use her hands and eyes to work out what she wants to do with the toy she is holding. It is better to give your child only a few selected items to play with at this age because she won't be able to concentrate on more than one thing at a time. A

stimulating, inviting environment is important for all creative play. Toys that are piled up in a jumble are not as inviting to a child as toys which are laid out for her in an attractive, inviting way.

SIX TO TWELVE MONTHS

Once your baby has learned to support herself sitting up and has started to make her first attempts at moving around, she will want toys that she can manipulate. This is the ideal time to give your child an activity centre with lots of different knobs and handles for her to twist and turn. By around seven or eight

months she will want to find out what things can do and will bang objects on the ground or table to find out if they make a noise or wave them in the air to see what happens. As her manipulative skills develop she will learn that she can use her hands and arms simultaneously and will start to bang things together. She will be able to reach out to you with both arms when she wants to be picked up. It takes a while longer for her to learn how to let go of items she is playing with, but you can encourage her by giving her an object, then holding out your hand and asking for it back. Once she's

A young baby will enjoy being read to from a simple board book and will be interested in touching the pages. She will soon learn how to recognize the book's pictures.

can put things back into the container and will spend ages tipping things out and putting them back again. She will try doing this with different objects and may discover that some of them don't fit. As your child plays she will be learning about the nature of the objects, how they behave, and their relative size and shape.

Water play can be introduced now and your baby will enjoy filling and emptying plastic beakers while she is having her bath. Give her toys which have different sizes of holes in them so that she can spend time sprinkling or pouring the water from one container into another.

Once your baby has started to crawl, give her toys that roll and move when they are pushed along so that she can go after them. Later, as she starts taking her weight on her legs, you can encourage her and help her balance with sturdy push-along toys, such as a brick trolley. This will

Your child will often put different things in her mouth to investigate them.

got the hang of this game she will keep you busy for hours!

As she becomes more mobile, your baby will want to be into everything and her natural curiosity could lead her into danger, so you need to pay constant attention to safety. One of your baby's favourite pastimes will be emptying things out of containers. She will take things out of cupboards with just as much enjoyment as she will empty shapes out of a shape sorter. Once she has emptied a container she will want to examine the contents in great detail and will bang things together and may put them in her mouth before discarding them and moving on to the next object. When she has mastered this she will soon learn that she

A baby walker will help your child to walk and some double as an activity centre.

give her something to hold onto until she feels confident enough to let go and walk unaided.

BOOKS

It is never too early to introduce your baby to books. Start at an early age with brightly coloured rag books that your baby can chew as well as handle, or simple board books. At first she will enjoy these books as objects to be explored but, if you sit her on your knee and talk to her about the pictures in the book, she will soon learn to recognize them. Encourage her involvement by making the noises of any animals pictured in the books and then getting her to do the same.

Games to play

• "Pat-a-cake, pat-a-cake, baker's man" is a rhyme to which your baby will enjoy clapping. When you get to "prick it and pat it and mark it with ..." use your baby's own initial and then her name when you come to "put in the oven for ...".

• Blowing bubbles using either a made-up solution and a wand or washing-up liquid and your hands.

• "Peek-a-boo": use your hands to cover your face; then later hide and seek: hide objects under a soft cloth for your baby to find.

• Hold your baby's hands securely and rock her gently backwards and forward while singing "Row, row, row the boat ...".

• Sit your baby on your knee facing towards you and hold her firmly by the hands as you bounce her in time to "Humpty Dumpty". When you get to the big fall allow your baby to drop through your knees while holding her firmly.

By just giving your baby one toy at a time to play with, she will be able to concentrate on it more fully.

Toys for 0-6 months
- Mobile.
- Rattle.
- Soft toys.
- Baby mirror.
- Squeaker.
- Baby gym.
- Play mat.

Toys for 7-12 months
- Cloth or card books.
- Big ball.
- Soft blocks.
- Beakers.
- Bath toys.
- Pop-up toys.
- Musical toys.
- Push-along toys.

Your young baby will enjoy looking at a toy hung from the pram or above the cot.

This rollaball can be rolled along and will help your baby's hand/eye co-ordination.

Simple toys which are colourful, tactile and chewable will interest a young baby.

As your baby learns to co-ordinate his hands, he will like to hold and feel toys that are easy to handle. This frog also has a baby-safe mirror. Your baby will be fascinated by his own reflection.

A play telephone with push buttons that make different noises will intrigue your baby and keep him amused for hours.

This colourful activity octopus has eight different-textured tentacles for your young baby to grasp and pull at. The caterpillar can be bent into different positions.

Your older baby will enjoy playing with different-sized, coloured stacking beakers.

This stacker has different coloured rings to help an older baby recognize colours and learn how to stack the rings.

This shape sorter offers your child the opportunity to explore different shapes as well as colours.

Once your baby can sit unaided he will enjoy toys such as this train that he can push along the floor.

A simple shape sorter will give your older baby hours of entertainment as he discovers how to put the squares into the holes and then watch them drop inside.

All babies enjoy an activity centre and one that can be fixed to the side of the cot will keep your baby amused when you put him down for a rest.

Pull-along toys will develop and encourage your baby's mobility. They will also help him gain confidence as he learns how to push and pull the toy back and forth along the length of the floor.

SOCIAL BEHAVIOUR

A newborn baby doesn't appear very sociable to the outside world because she doesn't smile or respond verbally until some weeks after birth. But her parents' reactions to the baby's ordinary behaviour lead to the development of social mannerisms. For example, wind may cause your baby to appear to smile at an early age and you respond by smiling back. Your baby will eventually realize that this movement of her mouth makes you react in this way and so will use it deliberately in the future. It is this early, simple form of communication that is the basis for your child's social development.

All babies' early social learning comes from imitating the people with whom they have the most contact, generally their mother and father. A newborn of only a few hours can imitate some adult gestures such as poking her tongue out or yawning. This ability to imitate is one of the most important tools your baby has to help her learn about life.

Through imitation your baby will eventually start communicating. You will speak to her and she will respond with "coos" and will wriggle her body in delight. This first stage of conversation will eventually develop into the ability to talk and listen. These early conversations often start during feeding, because the rhythm of feeding initiates your baby into the basics of dialogue. A baby sucks in her mother's milk in bursts with pauses in between. It is during these pauses that her mother usually fills in the gap by talking happily to her.

IMITATION BECOMES CHOICE
Social interaction between you and your baby becomes increasingly intentional on her part during the first two months of life, with much of your baby's behaviour geared towards making you react. These early conversations and the ability to imitate are just two ways of getting you to respond; the other very effective way is crying. Initially, your baby's cries are a reflex to pain, hunger, or discomfort. But crying assures a baby of adult response, especially her mother's. Her cries will increase her mother's heart rate and, if breast-feeding, her mother will automatically start producing milk. Within a few weeks a baby will have learned to expect certain reactions to her crying, such as being fed or picked up.

At around six weeks your baby will learn to smile properly, another social skill which she will be able to use to her advantage. Although her

When young babies are placed together, they don't play with each other as they haven't yet learned how to interact. Instead they will just play on their own.

If you put two or three babies together in a playpen they will not play together as they haven't learned how to socialize.

first smiles are simply facial grimaces, your response will be such that she soon discovers that by using her facial muscles in this way she is guaranteed to get you to smile back. A baby will quickly learn to repeat an action if she gets a positive reaction. However, if she regards the response she receives as negative she is less likely to repeat the action.

By three months your baby will be able to show her enjoyment of people and surroundings. She will respond to friendly adults and will generally not mind who is with her as long as they are paying attention to her. Your baby will enjoy activities such as having a bath and often show pleasure when she realizes that bathtime has arrived. Feeding will be a great source of emotional pleasure and your baby will study your face unblinkingly while she feeds.

At around four months your baby will cry more deliberately. She will

probably pause after crying to see if anyone is coming in response, before crying again. She has learned that crying brings attention and this new ability to manipulate is the beginning of some exciting discoveries.

CHANGING BEHAVIOUR PATTERNS
Somewhere after six months your child may change from a social, happy baby, who will go to anyone and reward complete strangers with smiles, to one who overnight has become wary of people she doesn't know. Your baby has reached the stage when she needs time and space to handle each new sight and sound; and a stranger may present her with too many new, unfamiliar things to be taken in at one time. This new wariness leads to what is known as stranger anxiety. It often manifests itself as loud protestations when your baby is about to be separated from you. She is at the stage of develop-

As your baby will feel safe with you, try to show her different toys and items to interest her and attract her attention.

ment when she is becoming increasingly sensitive to change and appears to be suddenly more dependent. She may try to avoid upsetting or stressful events by crying, clinging to you, or turning away from what is upsetting her. Towards the end of her first year she may start to use objects such as a favourite blanket, bottle, or thumb as a comforter.

Over the next six months your baby will probably show an increasing reticence with strangers but will be very responsive to people with whom she is familiar. She may become very clinging so that any separation from you is accompanied by real distress. This attachment may cause you problems, but it is in fact an important stage of development. Your baby now recognizes individuals as people and is beginning to develop selective, permanent relationships. She will use these relationships as a safe base from which to explore the world. Now that she is getting older, your baby will use her

A baby will sit with her brother because he is familiar. She will be interested in his toys but won't play with him.

developing vocal skills to create noise – this guarantees the attention that gives her the reassurance she needs. She may use mimicry to make you laugh and the more you show your appreciation the more she will repeat the antic which is amusing you. This is her first real control over her social environment.

By the time she is a year old, your child will probably have grasped the idea that she exists as an entity. She may even begin to use a word or

Your baby will sit quite happily on your knee, but may be wary of moving to his grandmother who is less familiar to him.

A baby will soon learn to recognize his older sister and will happily let her help him to stand up.

sound to describe herself as a means of expressing this. Her social skills, however, are still very limited and she will show little interest in anyone outside her immediate circle of well-known people. Other children hold very little appeal for your child at this age and are more likely to be treated as inanimate objects rather than playmates.

It will be another year or two before your child has enough social understanding to develop friendships with other toddlers.

How you can help

• Encourage your baby to imitate you by exaggerating your responses to her actions.

• Smile at your baby to let her know how pleased you are when she smiles at you.

• If she becomes wary of strangers don't force her to be sociable.

• When you have to leave your baby, say goodbye quickly; don't prolong the parting.

BABY MASSAGE

Touch is an important part of your baby's physical and emotional growth, and massage is an ideal way of extending your natural inclination to caress and cuddle your baby. Massage has been used on babies in India and Africa for hundreds of years, not only to help form a bond between mother and baby, but also as a means of relieving colic, helping the digestive system, and making the developing muscles supple. It is thought that gentle stroking encourages the abdominal walls to relax, which helps to alleviate wind and ease colicky pain; massaging the young limbs will also help to strengthen them.

There are a number of specific massage techniques that can be learned, but initially your instinctive touch will be enough, just as long as you are gentle and don't try to manipulate your baby's limbs. You need to be sensitive to your baby's moods and should only massage her

when she is content, perhaps between feeds or after a bath. Before you undress your baby for massage, make sure that the room is very warm and draught-free – this is important because babies lose their body heat 10 times more quickly than adults.

Remove any rings or bracelets before you begin and make sure that your fingernails are short and that there are no jagged edges that could scratch or irritate your baby. Relax your hands by stretching and shaking them, then warm them up by rubbing them together. Place a small amount of baby oil on your hands and, with your fingertips, gently massage the baby's skin using light, rhythmic movements. Start at the head and gradually work down to the feet.

Remember, a newborn needs only a feather-light, extremely gentle touch, and you must be careful when stroking the head and around

the still-healing navel. The tiny infant will naturally revert to the fetal position, so you shouldn't try to straighten out her arms and legs too much. As your baby gets older you can start to apply a slightly firmer touch, using the whole of your hand in the massage. When you have finished and your baby is dressed, allow her to have a sleep if that is what she seems to want.

Massaging tips

- Don't attempt to massage your baby if she is tired, hungry, or fretful.
- Allow yourself plenty of time so that the massage is not hurried or stressed.
- Get everything you need ready before you begin.
- Don't massage for more than 10 minutes or your baby will start to become bored.
- Talk or sing to your baby during the massage so that it is a pleasurable experience.
- If your baby isn't enjoying the massage, stop immediately and try again another time.

How to massage your baby

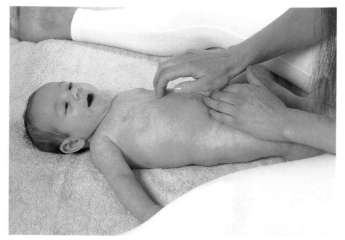

1 *Your baby will love the feel of massage. Place him on a towel in a warm room. Take some warmed baby oil into your hand and lightly massage his chest with circular movements.*

2 *Move on to the arms. Hold your baby's hand in one hand and with the other squeeze down his arm from the shoulder to the wrist. Repeat three times and then work on the other arm.*

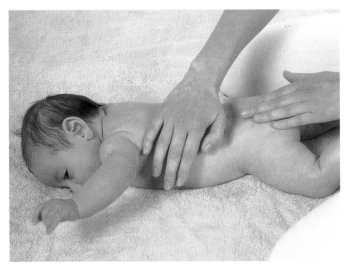

3 *Turn him onto his stomach and, with a hand on each side of his body, massage him from his bottom up to his shoulders, crossing your hands from side to side. Work down again and repeat.*

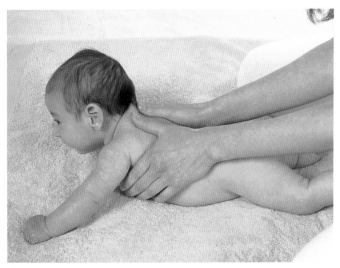

4 *Placing your hands on either side of his shoulders, bring your thumbs together and gently massage around your baby's neck and shoulders with a circular movement.*

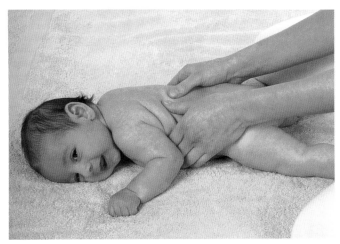

5 *Move both your hands down to your baby's left-hand side and softly knead his skin for a short time between your fingers. Repeat on his right-hand side.*

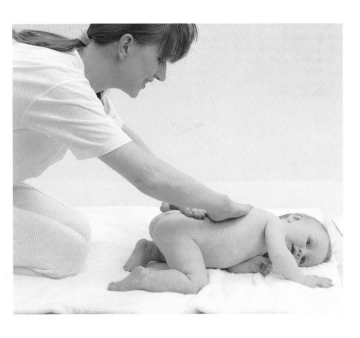

6 *Move your hands into the centre of your baby's back and do some light kneading movements with your fingers up and down the length of his spine.*

To finish your baby's massage, make some soft circling strokes with both hands up and down the back.

TRAVELLING WITH A BABY

The secret of successful travelling with children, no matter how long or short your journey, is careful planning. Young children are surprisingly adaptable, so providing that you take the essentials – food, nappies, and a favourite toy or two – your child should be quite happy to go with you.

The car is probably the easiest form of transport with a baby as you can use it as a kind of nursery on wheels, packing into it everything that you and your child are likely to require. Prepare a survival kit for the journey before you set off and keep it where it is easily accessible. The kit should include spare nappies, a change of clothes, baby wipes, changing equipment, and a mat or towel. If you are bottle-feeding or giving solids, you will also need to include some feeds plus some feeding equipment.

From birth your child should travel in the car in an approved safety restraint suitable for his age and weight. These restraints must be fixed and used properly to obtain maximum protection for your child in the event of an accident.

An older baby will need to be kept amused on the journey and the easiest way to do this is with a selection of toys. Choose toys that have been specially designed for use in the car, or ones which have suction pads that will stick on the window or the back of the front seat. These are better than loose toys, which you may find you have to retrieve each time they are dropped.

Try to make the journey as relaxed as possible by checking the route before you set out and allowing extra time to get there. This way you won't arrive late and anxious because you've had to make a number of unscheduled stops. If you are going on a long journey consider travelling at night. If you are fortunate, your child will be soothed by the motion of the car and will sleep for at least half the journey.

If the journey you are taking involves public transport, you will need to be selective about what you take with you as you'll have to transport your luggage as well as your baby. Take a similar survival kit to the one already mentioned, but make sure it is packed into an easy-to-carry holdall. If possible, take a lightweight pushchair, which you can fold with one hand, leaving the other free, or put your baby in a baby carrier, either strapped on your front if he is still very young, or on your back if he is old enough to sit up on his own.

If you are booking a seat on a train, coach, or plane, always mention the fact that you are travelling with a young child when you arrange your ticket and ask for the most convenient seating accommodation available. If the rail or coach station has a lot of steps to be negotiated ask one of the staff to help you, or find out if there is a lift you can use.

Some airlines have sky cots and others will allow you to take a buggy onto the plane as hand luggage.

They may even allow you to use your car seat (if it is of a suitable type) as a restraint for your child. Ask the airline or your travel agent what facilities are available for babies and older children before you set off.

Whichever method of transport you use, always shield your child from the sun, and make sure that any exposed skin is protected by a high-factor sunscreen. Keep your baby as comfortable as possible by putting him in clothes that are loose and easy to change. A number of layers of fairly thin clothing are best as this will allow you to add or take away a layer depending on how warm it is. Cars can get very hot in the summer, with the temperature creeping up considerably without you realizing it, so keep a constant check on your child while travelling.

Once your baby can support his head, you can put him in a carrier on your back. But always make sure that it is a comfortable fit.

A baby sling is an ideal way for either parent to carry a young baby, both inside the house, or when they are out and about.

KEEPING YOUR CHILD SAFE

Although there is no such thing as a completely safe home, many accidents can be prevented by taking a few safety precautions. High-risk areas can be made safer by installing devices that have been specially designed to prevent your child getting into danger.

HALL, STAIRS AND LANDING
The most common accident in these constantly used corridor areas is a child falling down the stairs, so keep staircases blocked off at both the top and bottom.
What you can do:
• Ensure that there is no loose floor

Stairs can be hazardous for your child and should ideally be blocked off top and bottom. Teach him to hold on to the spindles or wall to keep his balance.

covering or any trailing wire at the top of the stairs on which either you or a child could trip.
• If you have carpet on the stairs make sure that it is securely fitted and in a good state of repair.
• Make sure that the gaps between the stair spindles are no more than 10cm/4 in so that a child's head cannot get stuck between them.
• Fix gates at the top and bottom of the stairs to prevent young children from having access to them.
• Check that the lighting is good, so that there is no risk of tripping on some unseen object on the stairs.
• Fit safety film or safety glass to any glass doors in these areas.
• Make sure that the front-door latch and letterbox are out of reach.

LIVING ROOMS
These rooms are more difficult to keep safe because the environment is constantly changing as people come in and out and items are moved. Frequent safety checks are needed because the danger areas change as your child becomes more mobile. Try looking at the room from your child's level. One of the biggest dangers in the living area is fire.
What you can do:
• Install a circuit-breaker.
• Install smoke alarms throughout your home.
• Fit all fires with guards.
• Use electrical plug socket covers to prevent a child poking something into the socket.
• Unplug electric fires when they are not in use.
• Make sure that all fabrics and upholstery are made from fire-resistant materials.
• Keep matches, lighters and cigarettes out of reach and regularly empty ashtrays.

A safety gate is an essential piece of baby equipment. Fitted to the top or bottom of the stairs it will prevent your baby from climbing the stairs and falling. Placed across a doorway it will keep your child out of a room, such as the kitchen, where he could be in danger.

As your baby becomes more mobile he will use anything he can hold on to when pulling himself up. Once he is standing, things that were safely out of the way while he was still only sitting or crawling can now be reached.

Ideally, don't smoke at all!
• Fit safety protectors to the corners of tables and cupboards.
• Use mats instead of tablecloths so that your child can't pull things off the table on top of her.
• Place all ornaments and breakables out of reach.
• Check the floor regularly for small objects that could be swallowed.

KITCHEN

This is potentially the most dangerous room in the house for a young child. The most common accidents to occur in the kitchen are scalds from hot water, burns from cookers, and poisoning from cleaning products. What you can do:
• Keep the doorway blocked with a safety gate so that your child can't get in unnoticed.
• Put all sharp objects, such as knives, well out of reach of children.
• Fit safety catches to all low-level

cupboards, drawers, the fridge, and also the freezer.
• Use a shortened coiled kettle flex.
• Cook on the back rings of the hob with the pan handles facing inwards.
• Use a pan guard on the cooker.
• Never leave containers of hot liquid, such as cups or pots of tea, where your child can reach them.
• Make sure that all household chemicals and cleaning materials are kept out of reach and that their lids are always tightly screwed on.

Kitchen cupboards have a fascination for most young children. Safeguard your child by fitting cupboards with safety catches so that he can't open them.

BATHROOM

Among the most common accidents to happen in the bathroom are scalds from hot water, falls in the bath or shower, poisoning from medicines, and cuts from razors, scissors and broken glass.
What you can do:
• Make sure that all medicines and other dangerous objects, such as razors, are locked away in a cabinet which is placed out of easy reach of a child.
• Use a non-slip mat in the bottom

of the bath to prevent your child from slipping.
• Fit a lock to the toilet seat.
• Make sure that your child cannot reach the bathroom window by climbing on the toilet or the bath.
• Always run cold water into the bath before adding hot water and then check the temperature before putting your child into the tub.
• Make sure the hot water thermostat is not too high. The water should not be above 32°C/90°F.
• Hang a towel over the taps to prevent a child burning herself.
• Check that a child can't reach the door lock and lock herself in.

NURSERY

This is the one room where a child will spend time alone, so regular

---

Equipment

• Make sure any equipment you buy conforms to the safety regulations established by the European Union (EU) and the British Standards Institute (BSI).
• Only use equipment for the age of the child it has been designed for.
• Second-hand equipment needs to be checked thoroughly for safety.
• Always use safety straps when you put your baby in a pram, pushchair, highchair, or bouncing cradle.
• Never put a bouncing cradle on a raised surface because your baby's active movements could easily make it fall off.
• When travelling in a car, always put your baby in a car seat approved for the child's weight and age.
• Use child locks on the doors.
• Don't leave your child alone in the car, even if she is firmly strapped into her seat.

safety checks need to be carried out as your child grows and becomes more adventurous.

What you can do:

• Make sure that your baby's cot and mattress conform to safety standards and that the mattress fits snugly into the cot base.

• If your child sleeps in a bed, always use a bed barrier and make sure there is a safety gate fitted at the top of the stairs.

• Use a cot light, nursery light, dimmer, or plug light to give your child reassurance at night and to allow you to look in on her without causing any disturbance.

• Install a nursery listening device so that you can monitor your child.

• Place a thermometer in the nursery to help you keep a check on the temperature. The room needs to be around 18°C/65°F.

• If you, or your partner, must smoke, protect children from coming into contact with cigarette smoke, which could put them at risk from coughs, chest infections, and even cot death. There is also some evidence linking passive smoking with the development of childhood asthma.

• Fit any windows with locks.

• Make sure you place the cot or bed away from the window.

OUTSIDE

Many accidents happen outside the home. Even if you have your own garden you should never leave a young child outside unattended.

What you can do:

• Keep all garden tools and chemicals locked away.

• Fit locks to garden sheds and garage doors.

• Make sure that the gate to the road outside is secure.

• Always use a harness and reins, or a wrist link, when you are out on the pavement with your child.

• Make sure that the surface under any play equipment is safe for children to fall on.

• Cover up a pond or a water butt.

A bouncing cradle can be used from around three weeks, and your baby will enjoy reclining in the soft fabric seat. He will quickly learn that by kicking his legs hard he can make the cradle bounce.

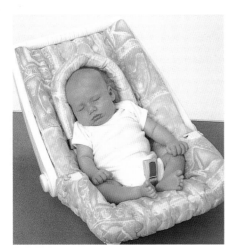

Many infant carriers double as car safety seats for at least the first six months. They are usually light and portable so that a newborn will fit into them snugly.

The rear-facing infant carrier can be fitted on both the front passenger seat and the rear seat. The seat is held in place in the car with any approved three-point adult seat belt.

FIRST AID

Many accidents can be dealt with when and where they occur. Adults with a sound knowledge of first aid can not only calm a distressed child, but they can also help to limit the effects of an accident, aid recovery, and could save a child's life. First of all you need to assess the situation and establish whether basic first aid is sufficient to treat the injury, or whether you think professional help might be required.

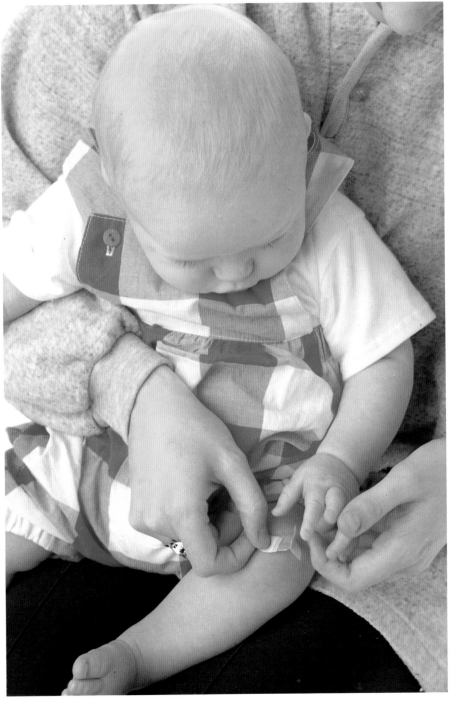

Any minor cuts that a young baby suffers usually can be dealt with on the spot from your first aid box.

GETTING MEDICAL HELP

If your child is unconscious or you think that he may have suffered spinal injury, after a fall, for example, always call an ambulance. If there is even a small possibility of spinal injury, do not attempt to move your child as this could cause severe damage. The best thing you can do is to keep your child warm, still, and calm until the ambulance arrives.

Time is of the essence in dealing with an emergency case that requires immediate medical attention. Should you need to get your child to the hospital urgently, and he can be moved safely, it may be quicker to take him there yourself. If possible, find someone else to drive, so that you can sit with your child in the back seat and give first aid if required. Although it is difficult, it is most important that you try to remain calm and to reassure your child. If you are unsure where the nearest hospital emergency department is, however, or have no suitable transport, then you should call an ambulance; the driver will quickly take you to the nearest suitable hospital.

If you fear that your child has injured his neck or back, call an ambulance and do not move him unless he is in immediate danger. If your child must be moved, you need extra pairs of hands to help turn him onto his back in one movement while holding his neck, shoulders and hips steady.

BREATHING

If your child has stopped breathing, start resuscitation at once and continue until breathing resumes. Get someone else to call an ambulance.

Mouth-to-mouth resuscitation:

1 Position – lay your baby or child on his back on a firm surface.

First aid kit checklist

It is important to have a fully stocked first aid kit in your home and you should also carry a basic kit in the car. You can buy ready-made kits, or you can make up your own by buying the items separately and storing them in an airtight container, out of the reach of children. You should check the contents regularly and replace items as they are used, so that you will always be ready for an emergency. Your home first aid kit should contain:

- assorted plasters.
- cotton wool.
- sterile gauze dressings.
- sterile eye pad.
- roll of 5 cm/2 in gauze bandage.
- crepe bandages.
- triangular bandage.
- safety pins.
- surgical tape.
- scissors.
- blunt-ended tweezers.
- paracetamol syrup.
- antiseptic solution or wipes.
- calamine lotion.
- clinical thermometer or fever strip.
- doctor's telephone number.
- details of your nearest hospital casualty department.

4 Check breathing – once his airway is open he may breathe spontaneously. Place your ear near the mouth and look along the body for movement. If there is no breathing after five seconds, give artificial ventilation.

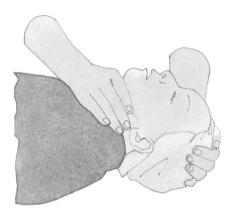

5 With a baby, cover his nose and mouth with your lips and breathe gently into his lungs until the chest rises. With a child, tilt his head back and bring the chin forward. Pinch his nostrils, take a deep breath and seal your lips around the child's mouth. Blow steadily until his chest rises.

6 Monitor recovery – your child's chest should rise as you blow air into the lungs, and fall when you take your mouth away. Look for this each time you raise your head to take a new breath of air. The first two breaths should be given quickly, then

2 Clear his airway – tilt his head on its side and remove any obstruction from the mouth with your fingers.

3 Open his airway – if your child is unconscious the airway may be blocked or narrowed, making breathing difficult or impossible. With a baby, tilt his chin using one finger. With a child, place one hand on the forehead, pushing his head backwards while you tilt his chin gently with the other hand.

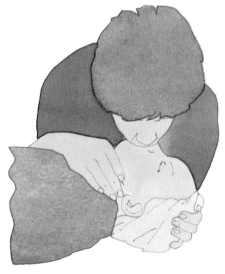

continue at a rate of one breath every three seconds. Keep this up until a medically qualified person can take over.

If your child's chest fails to rise the airway may not be fully open, so readjust the position of his head and jaw and try again. Check a baby's pulse on his upper arm. With a child, check the pulses in his neck or groin. If the heart is not beating, external chest compression is needed.

EXTERNAL CHEST COMPRESSION

If your baby is under one year old and you can't feel a pulse or hear a heartbeat, start chest compressions:

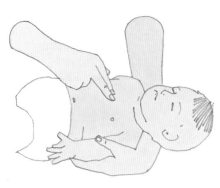

1 Place two fingers on the middle of your baby's breastbone, just below the nipples. (Use the heel of your hand on an older child.)

2 Press your fingers 1.3 cm/½ in into his chest five times in three seconds, making the compressions smooth and rhythmic.

3 Give a breath into his lungs and then five more chest compressions.

4 Continue with five compressions followed by one breath until the heart starts beating, or emergency help arrives.

5 Check every few minutes to see if the heart has started beating. When it does start you must stop the chest compressions immediately.

6 Continue with artificial respiration until your baby begins to breathe on his own.

UNCONSCIOUSNESS AND THE RECOVERY POSITION

If a baby is unconscious but breathing, cradle him in your arms, tilting his head so that his airway is kept open, and phone for medical help. An older child should be put in the recovery position. This prevents your child's tongue from slipping back into his throat and obstructing his airway, and avoids choking if he vomits. Put your child into this position if unconscious, but still breathing:

1 Lie your child on his back, face turned towards you, keeping the chin pulled down.

2 Place the arm near you at right angles to his body, elbow bent, with the palm upwards.

3 Fold the other arm over your child's chest with the back of his hand against his opposite cheek.

4 Lift the furthest knee, keeping this foot flat on the ground.

5 Keeping your child's hand pressed against his cheek, pull on the thigh furthest away from you, to roll him towards you.

6 Tilt your child's head back with his hand supporting it. Adjust his upper leg so that it supports his body.

7 Cover the child with a blanket and stay with him until help arrives, checking constantly for breathing and heartbeat.

CUTS AND GRAZES

You should seek medical help if there is a serious risk of infection, even with small wounds. But treat minor wounds yourself:

1 Clean the wound and surrounding area under running water.

2 Use an antiseptic cream or saline solution to reduce the risk of infection.

3 Apply a plaster or dressing once the surrounding area is dry.
Never:
• use a tourniquet.

Larger, more serious wounds must be treated immediately to control the bleeding and to minimize the risk of infection. Once the blood flow has been stemmed you should take your child to hospital:

1 Control any severe bleeding by applying direct pressure to the wound. If possible use an absorbent sterile dressing.

2 If the wound is on an arm or leg, raise and support it.

3 Cover the wound with a sterile dressing and attach it firmly with a bandage or adhesive tape to help control the bleeding.

BURNS AND SCALDS

Burns are caused by dry heat like flames and hot electrical equipment. Scalds are the result of wet heat, such as steam or boiling water. There is always a risk of infection with both burns and scalds because of the damage they do to the skin.

1 Cool the damaged area of skin under running cold water for at least 10 minutes.

2 Try to remove anything that might constrict the area if it swells, for example, rings or tight clothing.

3 Cover with a sterile dressing.

4 Always seek medical advice for all minor burns and scalds.

Never:

• apply butter, oil or grease to the damaged area.

• burst any blisters.

• use adhesive dressings or tape.

• remove anything that is sticking to the burn.

BRUISES AND SWELLING

If your child falls and hits himself, or receives a blow, bleeding may occur under the skin that causes swelling and discoloration. This should fade over about a week. You should hold a cloth that has been wrung out in cold water, or wrapped around an ice pack, to the bruised area for about half an hour to help reduce the swelling.

STRAINS AND SPRAINS

A strain is a tear or rupture of a muscle which causes swelling and discomfort. However, a sprain is more serious because it involves damage to the joint itself or the ligaments that surround it. Symptoms of a sprain include swelling, acute pain, and restricted movement. Both strains and sprains require the same treatment:

1 Avoid any activity that may overstrain the injured area until the swelling has gone down. Do not massage the injury because this may cause further damage.

2 Cool the injury with a cold pack, a bag of ice wrapped in a towel, or a cold, wet towel. This will reduce the pain and control inflammation.

3 Use a bandage to apply gentle compression to the injured area. This will give support and help to lessen inflammation.

4 Raise and support the injured area as this will help reduce swelling.

APPLYING A BANDAGE

Select the width of bandage appropriate to the area to be covered.

1 Support the injured limb while you are bandaging.

2 Start below the injury site, and wrap the bandage around the limb, using a spiral action, overlapping by two-thirds each time.

3 Secure with a safety pin or some adhesive tape.

4 Check to make sure that the bandage isn't restricting the circulation.

5 Bandage injured joints by wrapping the bandage around the joint in a figure-of-eight pattern, overlapping by two-thirds each time.

Never:

• bandage too tightly because this can affect the circulation. If the fingers or toes of the bandaged limb are cooler or darker than the other limbs the bandage is too tight. It should be removed and then reapplied, fixing it in position more loosely.

• ignore a limb injury. Always seek medical help if the leg is too painful to take your child's weight, if he is not using his arm, or if any swelling hasn't gone down after 48 hours.

BROKEN BONES

Technically, a broken or cracked bone is a fracture. All fractures should be treated with great care because any undue movement could cause further damage:

1 Keep your child still and cover with a coat or blanket.

2 Remove anything which might constrict any swelling around the injured area.

2 Get medical assistance.

BITES AND STINGS

Bites from mosquitoes and midges or stings from wasps and bees can be extremely painful, causing hard, red,

swollen lumps which itch intensely. A small number of people are allergic to wasp and bee stings. If your child appears to be having difficulty breathing as the result of a sting you must seek medical help immediately. In ordinary circumstances:

1 If the sting has been left in the skin, remove it with tweezers, taking care not to squeeze the poison sack because this would force the remaining poison into the skin.

2 Apply a cold compress to the site for quick relief from pain.

3 Massage sting-relief cream into the area for longer-term relief.

EYE INJURIES

Eyes are delicate organs which can be damaged very easily, so immediate first aid treatment is required if an injury occurs:

• Remove any foreign object from your child's eye using a damp piece of cotton wool. If you can't do this or the pain remains after removal, cover the eye with a clean pad and then take your child to hospital.

• If your child's eye has been injured by a blow, apply a sterile dressing, and take him to hospital for immediate treatment.

• Chemicals that are splashed into the eye should be washed out completely by flooding the eye with some clean, cold water for at least 15 minutes. Then cover the damaged eye with a clean pad and get your child to hospital.

CHOKING

This happens when a foreign object gets lodged in the throat and obstructs the airway.

For a baby:

1 Lay your baby face downwards, with the chest and abdomen lying

Choking

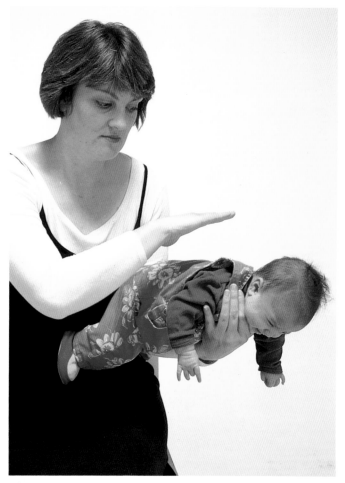

If your baby is choking, you will need to take immediate action. Lay a young baby face down with her chest and abdomen lying along your forearm with your hand supporting her head. Slap her gently on the back several times.

With an older baby or toddler the action would be slightly different. You will need to lay her horizontally, with her head facing downward. To remove the obstruction, slap her firmly between the shoulder blades.

along your forearm and your hand supporting his head.

2 Slap him gently on the back.

Note: if your baby or child doesn't start breathing normally once the blockage is completely removed, call an ambulance and begin artificial ventilation immediately.

For a child:

1 Lay your child across your knee, with his head down, and slap him sharply and firmly between the shoulder blades.

2 If the above fails to remove the blockage, use your finger to try to hook out the object, taking care not to push it further down your child's throat.

CROUP

Croup is a noisy barking cough which may be accompanied by fever and, in severe cases, your child may breathe with a grunting noise called "stridor". Croup can be quite frightening for both you and your child, so it is very important to stay calm and to reassure him. To help remedy the situation:

• Treat simple croup with warm drinks and paracetamol syrup to bring down any fever.

• Ease severe croup by getting your baby or child to inhale steam from a kettle, or sit near a running hot tap in the bathroom or near wet towels over a radiator. Make sure that he

cannot scald himself on the source of the steam.

• If your child is very distressed or has trouble breathing or swallowing, call your doctor immediately, or take him to hospital.

DROWNING

If possible get your child out of the water straightaway, otherwise you will need to give emergency first aid in the water.

1 Empty your child's mouth and, if his breathing has stopped, start to give him mouth-to-mouth ventilation. Do not attempt to remove any water out of your child's stomach or from his lungs.

2 If you carry your child, keep his head lower than the rest of his body to reduce the risk of him inhaling any water.

3 Lay him down on a coat or blanket. Open the airway and check his breathing and pulse.

4 Once your child is breathing normally again, remove all his wet clothes and cover him with some warm, dry ones. Give him a reviving hot drink.

5 Always take him to hospital for a thorough check-up, even if he appears to be fine and to have completely recovered.

ELECTRIC SHOCK

Most electrical accidents occur in the home, so it is vitally important to ensure that household appliances are wired correctly and kept out of the reach of young children. Severe injuries and even death can result from electric shock. But if a shock does still occur:

1 Switch off the current and pull out the plug before touching the child. If this is not possible, use something wooden, such as a broom handle or chair that will not conduct the electricity, to move him right away from the power source.

2 Check his breathing and heartbeat. If your child is unconscious, immediately place him in the recovery position.

3 Treat any burns.

4 Cover your child to keep him warm and reassure him by talking to him calmly.

5 Phone to get some medical assistance immediately.

Never:
• touch your child until the power source has been turned off.
• apply water to a burn that occurs from an electric shock while your

child is still attached to the source of the electricity.

NOSEBLEEDS

Bleeding often follows a blow to the nose, or may occur as a result of blowing the nose too hard. Sometimes there is no apparent reason for the nosebleed. The flow of blood can be quite heavy, which can be frightening, although it is not usually a serious problem:

1 Sit your child upright with his head positioned slightly forward. Putting the head back can sometimes cause choking and cause some discomfort.

2 Get your child to breathe through his mouth while you pinch the soft part of his nose firmly for 10 minutes until the flow of blood slows down and stops.

3 If your child's nose is still bleeding, hold a very cold cloth or an ice pack wrapped in a cloth to his nose for a couple of minutes, then pinch his nose again.

4 Try to ensure that your child avoids blowing his nose for several hours after a nosebleed has finally been staunched.

POISONING

This occurs when harmful substances are inhaled or swallowed. It is important to keep all such substances out of reach of young children. Always be on the alert and see that your child does not eat any poisonous berries or plants in the garden, or when you are out in the countryside. If you suspect poisoning, ring for an ambulance and then take immediate action:

1 Check breathing and be ready to resuscitate if necessary.

2 If your child is breathing, but is unconscious, place him in the recov-

ery position and phone for help.

3 If his lips or mouth show signs of burning, cool them by giving water or milk to sip slowly.

4 Keep the bottle or container the poison was in, or a similar berry or fruit to take to the hospital. This will enable the medical staff to administer the correct antidote to your child as fast as possible.

Never:
• try to give fluids to your child if he is unconscious.
• try to make your child sick. This can be extremely dangerous as the poison could find its way into his lungs and cause severe damage to these organs as well as endangering his breathing.

SHOCK

Severe bleeding, burns, and even fear can bring about a state of shock. You can recognize shock by an extreme loss of colour along with cold and clammy skin. The child may also be shivering and sweating at the same time. This may be accompanied by rapid breathing and dizziness, and possibly by vomiting. Shock often occurs after a major accident, so all casualties must be treated for shock, even if they are not showing any of these symptoms. In extreme cases shock can be fatal, so it requires some immediate action and should always be taken seriously:

1 Lay your child down on his side and make sure that his breathing isn't restricted.

2 Loosen any restricting clothing at his neck, chest, and waist. Then cover your child with a blanket or a coat, but take care not to allow him to overheat.

3 Try to get your child to remain still and to be calm while you seek medical help.

USEFUL ADDRESSES

There is no need to feel alone in the months after the birth.
The organizations mentioned below are happy to offer help and support to anyone who contacts them.
Remember to enclose an SAE when writing to them.

ANTE-NATAL AND BIRTH

Active Birth Centre, Bickerton House, 25 Bickerton Road, London N19 5JT.
Tel: 0171-561 9006

Association for Improvements in the Maternity Services (AIMS), 40 Kingswood Avenue, London NW6 6LS.
Tel: 0181-960 5585

Association of Radical Midwives (ARM), 62 Greetby Hill, Ormskirk, Lancs. L39 2DT.
Tel: 01695-572776

BLISS (Information for parents of special-care babies), 17-21 Emerald Street, London WC1N 3QL.
Tel: 0171-831 9393

British Pregnancy Advisory Service (BPAS), Austy Manor, Wootton Wawen, Solihull, West Midlands B95 6BX.
Helpline: 01564-793225

Foresight (The Association for the Promotion of Conceptual Care), 28 The Paddock, Godalming, Surrey GU7 1XD.
Tel/fax: 01483-427839. Contact at least four months prior to planned conception.

Foundation for the Study of Infant Deaths (Cot Death Research & Support), 14 Halkin Street, London SW1X 7DP.
Tel: 0171-235 0965
24-hour helpline: 0171-235 1721

Independent Midwives Association, Nightingale Cottage, Shamblehurst Lane, Botley, Hants. S032 2BY.
(No phone number, but please send A5 SAE for register of independent midwives)

Maternity Alliance, 15 Britannia Street, London WC1X 9JN.

Tel: 0171-837 1265 (Mon, Tues, Thurs, Fri 9am–1pm. Wed 2pm–5pm)

The Miscarriage Association, c/o Clayton Hospital, Northgate, Wakefield, W. Yorks. WF1 3JS.
Tel: 01924 200799 (answerphone out of office hours)

National Childbirth Trust (NCT), Alexandra House, Oldham Terrace, London W3 6NH.
Tel: 0181-992 8637

Stillbirth and Neonatal Death Society (SANDS), 28 Portland Place, London W1N 4DE.
Tel: 0171-436 7940
Helpline: 0171-436 5881
(10am–5.30pm)

Toxoplasmosis Trust, 61-71 Collier Street, London N1 9BE.
Helpline: 0171-713 0599

WellBeing (Health Research Charity for Women and Babies), 27 Sussex Place, Regent's Park, London NW1 4SP.
Tel: 0171-262 5337

FAMILY LINKS

Gingerbread, 49 Wellington Street, London WC2E 7BN.
Tel: 0171-240 0953

Meet a Mum Association, 14 Willis Road, Croydon, Surrey CR0 2XX.
Tel: 0181-665 0357. Also post-natal depression and general advice.
Helpline: 0181-656 7318.

National Childminding Association 8 Masons Hill, Bromley, Kent BR2 9EY.
Tel: 0181-464 6164

National Council for One Parent Families, 255 Kentish Town Road, London NW5 2LX.
Tel: 0171-267 1361

Working for Childcare, 77 Holloway Road, London N7 8JZ.
Tel: 0171-700 0281

SPECIAL NEEDS

ASBAH (Association for Spina Bifida and Hydrocephalus), 42 Park Road, Peterborough PE1 2UQ.
Tel: 01733 555988

British Diabetic Association, 10 Queen Anne Street, London W1M 0BD.
Tel: 0171-323 1531

British Epilepsy Association, Anstey House, 40 Hanover Square, Leeds LS3 1BE.
Free helpline: 0800 309030

Cystic Fibrosis Trust, Alexandra House, 5 Blyth Road, Bromley, Kent BR1 3RS.
Tel: 0181-464 7211

Down's Syndrome Association, 155 Mitcham Road, London SW17 9PG. Tel: 0181-682 4001

Galactosaemia Support Group, 31 Cotysmore Road, Sutton Coldfield B75 6BJ.
Tel: 0121-378 5143

Mencap (Royal Society for Mentally Handicapped Children and Adults), 123 Golden Lane, London EC1Y 0RT.
Tel: 0171-454 0454

National Asthma Campaign,
Providence House, Providence Place,
London N1 0NT.
Tel: 0171-226 2260
Helpline: 0345 010203
(Mon to Fri 9am–9pm)

National Autistic Society,
276 Willesden Lane, London
NW2 5RB. Tel: 0181-451 1114

National Deaf Children's Society,
15 Dufferin Street, London EC1Y 8PD.
Tel: 0171-250 0123

National Eczema Society,
163 Eversholt Street, London
NW1 1BU.
Tel: 0171-388 4097

**Research Trust for Metabolic
Diseases in Children (RTMDC),**
Golden Gates Lodge, Weston Road,
Crewe CW1 1XN.
Tel: 01270 250221

**Royal National Institute for the
Blind (RNIB),** 224 Great Portland
Street, London W1N 6AA.
Tel: 0171-388 1266

Scope (formerly Spastics Society), 12
Park Crescent, London W1N 4EQ.
Tel: 0171-636 5020

SENSE (National Deaf-Blind and Rubella
Association), 11-13 Clifton Terrace,
Finsbury Park, London N4 3SR.
Tel: 0171-272 7774

Sickle Cell Society, 54 Station Road,
Harlesden, London NW10 4UA.
Tel: 0181-961 7795 (Mon to Fri
9am–5pm)

**Voluntary Council for Handicapped
Children**, 8 Wakley Street, London
EC1V 7QE.
Tel: 0171-843 6000

FOR NEW PARENTS
**Association of Breastfeeding
Mothers**, 26 Holmshaw Close, London

SE26 4TH.
Tel: 0181-778 4769

Association for Post-Natal Illness,
25 Jerdan Place, London SW6 1BE.
Tel: 0171-386 0868
(answerphone out of office hours)

Cry-sis, BM Cry-sis, London WC1N
3XX (Counsellors available between
9am–11pm)
Tel: 0171-404 5011

La Leche League of Great Britain,
PO Box BM 3424, London WC1N
3XX.
Tel: 0171-242 1278. Helps and supports
women who wish to breast-feed. (24-
hour counselling service)

FAMILY WELFARE
Action for Sick Children, Argyle
House, 29-31 Euston Road,
London NW1 2SD.
Tel: 0171-833 2041 (Mon to Fri
9am–5pm)

Children's Legal Centre,
The University of Essex, Wivenhoe
Park, Colchester, Essex CO4 3SQ.
Tel: 01206 873820

Citizen's Advice Bureau,
address and telephone number for
your nearest office in your local telephone book.

Compassionate Friends, 53 North
Street, Bristol BS3 1EN.
Helpline: 0117 953 9639 (Mon to Fri
9.30am - 5pm)

Contact-a-Family, 170 Tottenham
Court Road, London W1P OHA.
Tel: 0171-383 3555

Cruse (Bereavement Care),
Cruse House, 126 Sheen Road,
Richmond, Surrey TW9 1UR.
Bereavement line: 0181-332 7227
(Mon to Fri 9.30am–5pm)

Family Planning Association, 27-35
Mortimer Street, London W1N 7RJ.
Tel: 0171-636 7866

Family Welfare Association,
501-505 Kingsland Road, London
E8 4AU.
Tel: 0171-254 6251

**National Association for the Welfare
of Children in Hospital (NAWCH),**
Argyle House, 29-31 Euston Road,
London NW1 2SD.
Tel: 0171-833 2041

**National Childcare
Campaign/Daycare Trust**, 4 Wild
Court, London WC2B 4AU.
Tel: 0171-405 5617

**National Society for the Prevention
of Cruelty to Children (NSPCC),**
National Centre, 42 Curtain Road,
London EC2A 3NH.
Tel: 0800 800 500
(free 24-hour confidential helpline)

Relate (National Marriage Guidance),
Herbert Gray College, Little Church
Street, Rugby, Warks CV21 3AP, or
look in telephone directory under "R"
for Relate or "M" for Marriage Guidance.

SAFTA (Support after termination for
abnormality), 73-75 Charlotte Street,
London W1P 1LB.
Tel: 0171-631 0285

Samaritans,
Tel: 0345 909090 (24-hour confidential
helpline). For local number look in your
telephone directory.

Smokers' Quitline,
Tel: 0171-487 3000

**Twins and Multiple Births
Association (TAMBA)**, PO Box 30,
Little Sutton, South Wirral L66 1TH.
Tel: 0151-348 0020 (Mon to Fri
9am–1pm)

Vegetarian Society,
Parkdale, Dunham Road, Altrincham,
Cheshire WA14 4QG.
Tel: 0161 9280793

INDEX

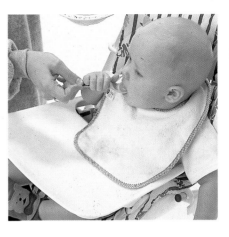

ACKNOWLEDGEMENTS

The author and publisher would like to thank the many individuals who helped in the creation of this book. In particular thanks are due to Bobbie Brown, Elsa Jacobi, Pauline Richardson, Mary Lambert and Jane Barret. Many thanks also go to everyone who modelled for special photography: Yvonne Adams and Martin; Ruth Auber and Bethany; Jo Bates and Lois; Amanda Bennet-Jones; Kim, Neil and Andrew Brown; Christine Clarke; Jacqueline Clarke and Cassia; Jocelyn Cusack and Beth; Sam Dyas and Colt; Patricia Gannon and Matthew; Nici Giles and Fergus; Yiota Gillis and Cameron; Sandra Hadfield and Annie; Louise Henriques and Joshua; Lynette Jones and Hugh and Rhys; Karen, Mark, Megan and Robert Lambert; Claire Lehain and Harriet; Lavinia Mainds and Polly; Pippa Milton and Oliver; Philippa Madden and Inca; Jackie Norbury; Jess Presland; Katey Steiner; Saatchi Spracklen and Niamh; Sophie Trotter and Archie; Josephine Whitfield and Lily May; Lucinda Whitrow and Hector. Thanks also to companies who loaned items and photographs: Blooming Marvellous Ltd (pages 38-39), Boots Children's Wear and Toys, Fisher-Price, Littlewoods Home Shopping, Maclaren Ltd and Mattel UK Ltd.